Insider's
Singapore

TIMES BOOKS INTERNATIONAL
Singapore • Kuala Lumpur

In the same series
Frankfurt
Kuala Lumpur
Tokyo

© 1999 Times Editions Pte Ltd
© 2001 Times Media Private Limited

Front cover photo: Bes Stock
Photos by David Brazil

Published by Times Books International
an imprint of Times Media Private Limited
Times Centre
1 New Industrial Road
Singapore 536196
Fax: (65) 2854871 Tel: (65) 2848844
E-mail: te@tpl.com.sg
Online Book Store: http://www.timesone.com.sg/te

Times Subang
Lot 46, Subang Hi-Tech Industrial Park
Batu Tiga
40000 Shah Alam
Selangor Darul Ehsan
Malaysia
Fax & Tel: (603) 56363517
E-mail: cchong@tpg.com.my

National Library Board (Singapore) Cataloguing in
Publication Data

Brazil, David.
Insider's Singapore / by David Brazil.
– Singapore: Times Books International, 2001.
p. cm. ISBN : 981204762X

1. Singapore – History – Miscellanea.
2. Singapore – Description and travel.
I. Title.

DS599.7   959.57 – dc21   SLS2001025869

Printed in Malaysia
ISBN 981 204 762 X

For Agatha Koh, Miss Cuddles, Kitty,
Chalky and not forgetting Anak

Contents

Foreword

Wah, another book on Singapore's past – its history and its heritage? Enough already, why this one? Anyhow, who cares about a world where there was no Lycra, no push-up bras, no handphones, no Internet, no e-mail, no PC games, no karaoke, no cable TV, no digital TV, no microwave ovens, no Italian food, no Starbucks, no ERP, no Y2K and none of that virtual reality/IT stuff?

And who wants to dip back into a world of *kacang putih* men, 5-cent ice-balls, Silver Spoon coffee house, Magnolia milk bar, Sputnik hawker centre, Double Rabbit panties, Two Flying Babies toilet paper, Sakura Teng, Rita Chao, permanent waves, drive-in cinemas and all that nostalgic *Growing Up* stuff?

Well, what makes this forward-to-the-past book different is that it's not dry-dust history, long lists of names and dates to commit to memory as if at school, as if facing yet another exam. There are 30 standalone stories awaiting, they're lively – and they happened. Right here, in Singapore. The stories don't start with 1819, then work their way though the years before stopping yesterday. They cover all the major milestones along the way of Singapore's short but dense history. Yet there's no need to gobble them all at once, at one sitting.

They can instead be sampled bite-size, buffet-style. Dip in-and-out, as and when. What's more, they're all linked to a particular place or street or monument that's still here. And upon which, as they say, there hangs a tale. Or in a couple of cases, hangs a tail.

And even though the past can seem a safer place, almost a comfort zone for those of a certain age in these troubled times, these 30 stories are not insisting the past was a better place than the now, or the future. They simply set out to show how the here-and-now came to be. And no, it wasn't always easy. Sometimes it was downright tragic. But like life itself, there were some smiles, even laughs, along the way.

So, who is this book for? OK, probably not for those who regard 10 minutes ago as who-needs-it history, for whom snappy soundbites are the norm. But it is for those who want to know that little bit more, and who might well be surprised to find out there was that little bit more. For students who need treat this as a mugger's manual, with yet another exam to follow. For those visiting Singapore or staying here, for those who want to know Singapore a little bit better, for whose who love Singapore. And overall, for those who are simply curious about this fascinating, surprising little island.

There may also be those who'd like to wallow a bit in the past as a kind of comfort zone. For as BG (NS) George Yeo, Minister of Information and the Arts, put it: 'Memories are what give a place its charms … If we can infuse the land with memories, then we will not just be a hotel. We will be a land with memories, a land with a past – and a land with hope for the future.'

Well, there's plenty of warm memories and land-infusing stuff to come over the following pages. So, here endeth the sermon. May I now sincerely urge, as too many history teachers (East and West) didn't and don't: 'Enjoy!'

David Brazil
January 1999

The City
and
Chinatown

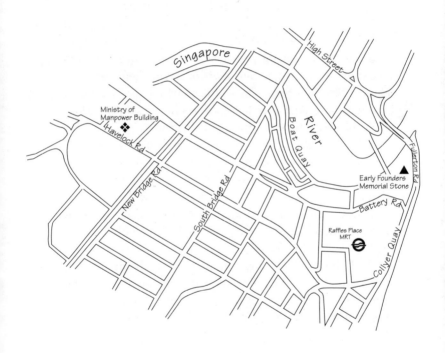

A Sadly Unfinished Monument

Early Founders Memorial Stone
Collyer Quay

*An admirable idea to honour the 'Unknown
Immigrant' of Singapore goes awry ...*

It was such a noble idea. But there it stands, merely a chunky
memorial stone topping off a pyramid-shaped chin-high
brick structure and now located on the street outside what was
the GPO and what is becoming the swish new Fullerton Hotel.

It was intended to be so much more. Even a keynote
memorial for the Singapore waterfront, with far more real
meaning than that Merlion. Instead, this dumpy-looking stone
only evokes what might have been. And who it was intended
to honour: the Early Founders or more poetically, the
'Unknown Immigrant'.

The idea was floated in 1969, that being the year of
Singapore's 150th anniversary. The instigator was the Alumni
International Singapore, a body set up to represent Singaporean
graduates of tertiary educational institutions from 11 countries
who had gathered here for that 150th anniversary.

Some $250,000 would be collected, it was boldly
announced, for a memorial which would grace Queen Elizabeth
Walk by the Padang. An open competition would be held.
Sculptors would be asked to come up with a design to celebrate
the Singaporean for his (and her!) 'courage, his adventurous
and enterprising spirit and his indomitable will, not only to
survive but to make good.'

Fine words, indeed. And so it came to pass that on the
Sunday morning of the 18 January 1970, Fullerton Road/
Collyer Quay was closed to traffic while the President of the
Republic, Yusof bin Ishak, laid the chunky granite stone,
suitably inscribed in the four official languages, on what was
supposed to be a temporary site.

Before an audience of some 500 people, including members of the diplomatic corps, President Yusof paid tribute to Alumni International for its 'imagination and initiative in erecting this memorial not to some legendary and doubtful hero, nor to some outstanding personality whom we can admire but with whom the ordinary man cannot identify, but to the ordinary nameless immigrants without whose labour and skill there would have been no modern Singapore.'

For All Who Created Modern Singapore

President Yusof had more stirring words about the proposed memorial: 'It carries no great names. In fact it has no names at all. It is for all men. It is not for the Chinese, the Indian, the Eurasian or any other single race. It is for all who in one way or another helped to create a modern multiracial, multicultural and multilingual Singapore.'

In short, the memorial would commemorate not just those for whom the dream came true but everyone who came here and made their contribution, no matter how modest, to the making of Singapore.

The first rumblings that all was not well emerged in July 1973. Designs for the memorial had been received from 38 sculptors, but the prize winners were not a happy bunch. For the top two **Controversy erupts ...** prizes were not awarded, no entry being deemed worthy of the honour. Instead, five sculptors received merit awards from Alumni International, together with a token $250.

As one of them, Ng Eng Teng (who was to receive Singapore's Cultural Medallion in 1981 and who now has his works all over the place), put it: 'We have never been so embarrassed or insulted in all our professional lives. No professional artist of our standing would condescend to receive such an amount. We felt we had been taken for a ride.'

In response, Alumni International expressed regret that the aggrieved sculptors had publicly stated their dissatisfaction. The body further rejected a complaint that the results were 10

The Early Founders Memorial Stone.

months overdue, and repeated that no suitable entry had been received.

Three of the five indignant 'prize-winning' sculptors were locals who had banded together to produce a design they described as 'four pieces of cuboid leaning towards each other and pivoted on four corners. Imagine how astounded we were when the entry was referred to as resembling "four chopsticks".'

Ironically, this was the nickname – and roughly the design concept – of the Memorial to the Civilian Victims of the Japanese Occupation, which went up in 1967.

In September 1975, the alumni went public again to record that the Early Founders project was at 'a very advanced stage and will be launched as soon as Government approval has been obtained. The site of the monument has already been earmarked on the reclaimed land off the Esplanade.'

It's at this stage that the story suddenly stops. It has emerged since that no design for the memorial had even been accepted in the first place. Plus, nothing close to the required $250,000 sum of money had been raised and that the ambitious plans had effectively been ditched. In 1985, the alumni announced that such money as had been gathered would be rediverted to other projects, such as providing scholarships.

And so it came to pass that the memorial stone became the memorial itself. It is tempting to observe that only if you are rich and famous will your memorial take shape and that if you are poor, you are many and you are anonymous, it may well not ...

The Benign Face of Empire

William Pickering and
the Chinese Protectorate

Havelock Road

'If there is any special genius in the British, it
is exemplified in Pickering, one of the real
founders of modern Singapore ...'

By 1870, immigrants from the southern reaches of China had made Chinese the majority population in Singapore. Yet Singapore's British authorities still had not a single official who could speak any of the relevant Chinese dialects. No one who could explain its political and judicial decisions. No one who could intervene in the distinctly laissez-faire approach the Chinese were taking towards opium, prostitution, gambling, slavery and various other vices.

Then one day in the London of 1871, Singapore's then governor, Sir Harry Ord (home on leave), came across William Pickering. Pickering astounded Ord by showing he could speak a whole range of relevant Chinese dialects. Hokkien, Teochew, Cantonese, Hakka, Foochew, even Mandarin – Pickering was fluent in them all. Recognising him as an official needed out East like few others, Ord offered him a job on the spot. In January 1872, William Pickering set off for Singapore.

He had learnt the dialects while serving a 10-year term in Hong Kong's Chinese Maritime Customs Service; now he would be Singapore's official interpreter. Just in time, too. Street fighting and gang riots had become the order of the day, and new legislation had just been brought in to register the secret societies at the heart of this Chinese lawlessness.

Pickering sat in the Singapore courtroom and was shocked to hear how its legal business was conducted. Chinese dialect translations of British edicts described Europeans as 'red-haired barbarians', judges as 'devils' and police as 'big dogs'.

Out on the streets, Pickering used an unusual tactic to calm disputes as and when they broke out: by producing his bagpipes (even if he was English rather than Scottish) and walking up and down as he played them. This sound and vision combo rarely failed to subdue Chinese onlookers. Pickering's sure command of dialects helped to sort out the secret society 'post office riots' between Teochews and Hokkiens over who had the right to send money and letters back to China.

In 1876, an official report into secret society activities was published. This uncovered how the coolie traffic (in reality, a slave trade) was carried out, and stressed how urgent action was required to intervene in the process. As things stood, many new arrivals at Boat Quay had been 'press-ganged' in their hometowns and forced to leave southern China ports in ships described as 'floating hells'. The space provided on board for each of them was just enough for them to lie down or if they were really unlucky, to squat. The live human cargo of one such notorious junkload was reduced by nearly half – from 400 to 220 – by the time it reached Singapore.

Once arrived, coolies were taken to houses described as 'not fit to keep pigs in'. Here they would be virtually locked in until employers were found for them. Sometimes the coolies were even frog-marched through town and onto other boats which would take them to neighbouring countries, where conditions were doubtless even worse than Singapore's.

Houses 'not fit to keep pigs in' ...

Protector and Friend

The major British recommendation in the 'coolie traffic' report was that each new arrival at Boat Quay should first encounter a British official who could speak his language and let the newcomer know that there was an 'officer of the Government whose special duty is to protect him and be his friend'.

In May 1877, William Pickering became the first such official under the title of Protector. He was based in a modest North Canal Road shophouse office known as the Chinese Protectorate.

During his 14 years in office, an estimated 700,000 Chinese immigrants arrived in Singapore. From the beginning, Pickering made it his business to board ships as they docked in Boat Quay, clear those who had paid their sea voyage fees and send others to government centres where employment contracts would be officially registered. For the abuses of this coolie trade had touched even the raw 19th century Singapore conscience and Pickering's opposition to the quayside presence of secret society agents looking out for their human 'cargo' received widespread public support.

In 1879, the Chinese Protectorate received and dealt with over 2,600 individual complaints from the public. Such complaints would earlier have been taken to a secret society for, often violent, satisfaction. Pickering devoted much of his enormous energy to extracting the sharp fingernails of these secret societies and when taking some welcome home leave in 1883, he received a handsome tribute from a group of prominent Chinese citizens for his work.

Cathouse-Bound

It was while checking the human contents of those vessels berthing at Boat Quay that Pickering became aware of another major problem – women. Their low numbers here and the sexual burdens on them (one estimate gave the ratio of one Chinese woman to 30 Chinese men) had resulted in the importation of women (plus fine-looking boys from Hainan island) for prostitution purposes.

Some 80% of newly-arrived Chinese women were immediately sold into brothels, then concentrated in the Kreta Ayer area. In 1881, at Pickering's instigation, the Contagious Diseases Ordinance was brought in, requiring all brothels and prostitutes to be registered with his Protectorate. This effectively legalised controlled prostitution. Pickering was realistic enough to know that the sexual imbalance would be dangerous if the cathouses were simply shut down.

Pickering divided Singapore's prostitutes into four categories:

✎ *those who had joined the trade voluntarily;*

✎ *those 'induced to leave China on the promise of good wages as seamstresses, nurses or hairdressers' and then immediately sold to brothels;*

✎ *those brought up as children in readiness for the trade; and*

✎ *those who had actually been born in brothels and who were thus regarded as the 'property' of that brothel-owner.*

Pickering took a hands-on approach to the issue. He insisted on seeing the women personally, one by one, to determine their exact circumstances. He left behind a written description of how this took place and the hysterical reaction it produced from the 'mama-sans' of the time.

'The inmates are every two or three months at uncertain intervals and at short notice called to the office, where they are carefully examined by the Registrar as to their condition and treatment. Every woman before being placed on the register is questioned, in the absence of the brothel-keeper or mistress, as to her willingness to be a prostitute.

'Some difficulty was experienced at first in making the keepers accept this innovation, as they plainly said they were afraid of losing the large sums invested in their girls. After threatening the law, riots, closing of shops, etc., and making a demonstration at the Protectorate in the shape of throwing back their licence boards, dancing on the floors in their wooden clogs and howling furiously, they found they must give in and are now reconciled to the measure as inevitable.'

As noted, the Protectorate did not actually prevent women from entering this line of work but simply tried to licence them. Soon, some 3,500 such women were on Pickering's books. This had an unplanned consequence as in 1888 alone, 1,218 'professional' women arrived from China, eager and willing to leap straight into the Singaporean fray. They'd heard the 'career opportunities' were good and at least somewhat protected here.

Good 'career opportunities' ...

For those women who didn't wish to follow the horizontal trade as a career, Pickering set up the Po Leung Kuk ('Home to Protect Virtue') in cooperation with prominent Chinese citizens. This expanding volume of work meant that the Protectorate needed bigger premises. In 1886, the first of five buildings the office used over the decades went up on the site now occupied by the Ministry of Manpower on Havelock Road/New Market Road.

When the Chips are Down ...

The third major strand of Pickering's work – control of illegal gambling – nearly brought about his demise, serving as a reminder that his work was at times extremely dangerous. On 18 July 1887, the then 37-year-old Pickering was sitting in the office dealing with the registration of the latest batch of female immigrants. Suddenly, a Teochew carpenter burst into the room. He stormed up to Pickering's desk and threw his iron axe at him, hitting the Protector full on the forehead with the wooden butt-end.

It took eight men to hold down the carpenter even if he kept insisting he had not meant to harm Pickering, merely to 'frighten' him. In November that year, the carpenter was given seven years' hard labour. The assumption was he had been set up by secret society members to warn Pickering to 'ease off' the anti-gambling side of his work.

Pickering's injury, though not fatal, was still a serious one and suspicion lingers that the Colonial Office used it as a means of edging Pickering out. For he had strenuously objected to new official attempts to completely outlaw the secret societies and, as he saw it, thereby losing control of 'the 165,000 registered members of Chinese Dangerous Societies' by driving them underground.

A doctor examined Pickering in 1889 and ruled that he was suffering from funny turns, during which he was 'unfit to undertake responsible business'. The doctor concluded: 'This morbid phase seems to have come on from the severe injury inflicted on his head when he was assaulted.' Pickering was forcibly retired in March 1890.

Forced retirement ...

He finally left Singapore in 1893, accompanied by a fanfare of tributes from most sections of the community. Especially from Chinese quarters which in fact petitioned for him to stay on in office. Perhaps the greatest tribute to his work was that no matter who subsequent Protectors were, the office continued to be called Pi-Ki-Ling among Singapore's Chinese. And the Malay term for the Protectorate was Pikring Punya Ofis.

Poor Pickering was not happy in his reluctant retirement. He declared himself unimpressed by manifestations of Chinese culture and, writing in a London magazine of 1895, observed that the Bible's *Book of Proverbs* had 'more wisdom than Confucius, Mencius and all the Chinese sages combined'. He also declared that British consuls in Chinese parts should not attempt to translate Chinese works of literature or philosophy. Instead, they should 'raise the character of our nation in the eyes of the conceited Chinese by translating such works as Shakespeare and Milton into the language of the Middle Kingdom ...'

In 1907, Pickering died in Italy; he was 67. A tribute paid to him by two British chroniclers of the era noted that Pickering was a rare exception to the British tendency to fill its empire-ruling classes mainly with the sons of its upper classes. They went on: 'If there is any special genius in the British, it is exemplified in Pickering, Protector of Chinese, one of the real founders of modern Singapore.'

Life After Pickering

Post-Pickering, the Protectorate still had much work to do. For example, in 1907, a 16-year-old Chinese girl, 'bought' for $230 as a maidservant, escaped from her cruel Chinese owners and found her way to the Protectorate. There she told how she worked from 5 am to midnight every day, and how the couple who owned her flogged her when angry, once hanging her up by her hair.

Another time when she put too much water in the rice she was cooking, her mistress stuck needles in her face. She had to shampoo her master and he would often keep her up all through the night to massage him, hitting her whenever she stopped. As proof, she showed Protectorate officers how her body was covered with sores, scars, rattan weals and ulcers. Her master fled Singapore, leaving his wife to face the music by serving a four-month jail stretch for the inhuman treatment of their slave.

The Protectorate continued until the 1942–45 Japanese Occupation, although its work between the two world wars tended more towards enforcing government restrictions on an increasingly anti-colonial population, censuring the newspapers and investigating political 'subversion'. And in such a way as to alienate the Chinese community so much that just before the fall of Singapore, the Chinese Chamber of Commerce and other august bodies petitioned the Governor to dismiss the Secretary of Chinese Affairs, as the Protector was now known.

These days, it is appropriate that on the other side of New Bridge Road from the Ministry of Manpower building, there is a Pickering Street. His name thus lives on, close to the spot where William Pickering conducted his humane endeavours on behalf of the downtrodden, the victimised, the degraded and the enslaved members of Singapore's Chinese community.

The Padang
and
Fort Canning

Orchard Rd

Bras Basah Rd

Victoria St

North Bridge Rd

Beach Rd

National Museum

Stamford Rd

Raffles Boulevard

Fort Canning Hill

'Chopsticks' Monument, War Memorial Park

City Hall MRT

Fort Canning Park

St Andrew's Cathedral

Padang

Connaught Drive

River Valley Rd

Hill St

Lim Bo Seng Memorial

Parliament House

Sir Stamford Raffles statue

South Bridge Rd

A Present from a King

Bronze Elephant
Parliament House, High Street

In 1871, Singapore became the
first-ever foreign country visited
by a reigning Siamese king ...

The most charming of Singapore's public memorials could easily be the black little brass elephant on its pedestal outside Parliament House on High Street. This elephant notes the visit here in March 1871 of the King of Siam (posthumously known as Rama V – conveniently also, because his full proper name was Somdetch Phra Paramindr Maha Chulalongkorn.)

The significance of this occasion was that Singapore thus became the first-ever foreign country visited by a reigning Siamese king. To be strictly accurate, Rama was then 18 years of age and was actually Siam's ruler only in name – it was not until 1888 that he took on the monarch's full powers in reality.

He stayed here for just over a week with his huge retinue. When the royal yacht Regent arrived to a rousing welcome from a military band and a troop parade along Battery Road (together with a gun salute from naval vessels in the harbour), it disgorged a total of 66 Siamese visitors, including two of the King's brothers, two ministers and many advisors, plus various womenfolk, flunkies and servants.

Their full programme for the week's 'package tour' here is unknown but it was recorded that on 18 March the King attended a flower show in the Botanic Gardens. Whatever else he got up to, he clearly enjoyed himself as he made several subsequent visits to Singapore. One such visit came in May 1880 when he arrived with his Queen and stayed at 'Siam House', the residence of the local Thai consul Mr Tan Kim Ching on North Bridge Road. It was while on this visit that the King made the then customary $1,000 donation to Tan Tock Seng Hospital.

The King and I

Rama V was the eldest of 67 offspring of his father, King Mongkut or Rama IV, who may be better known to the Western world as the first part of *The King and I*, that magnificent Rodgers & Hammerstein musical. Or more precisely as Yul Brynner, who made that part so much his own (it's a puzzlement that the original choice for the role was Rex Harrison!).

This musical is still banned in Thailand by decree of the Thai royal family, on the basis of its 'historical inaccuracies'. And because of its Western lack of reverence for the concept of monarchy that is so highly revered in Thailand? But mainly because of the prissy Englishwoman to whom the 'and I' part applies – Mrs Anna Leonowens, the governess who left Singapore in 1862 to spend eight years in Bangkok as tutor to the King and his multifarious offspring.

Her contract was not renewed and so needing cash, she turned to writing about her experiences and frankly, hamming them and 'exotic' Thailand up to boost sales by giving Western punters what she thought they wanted. What's more, the proper spelling of her family name was Owens, not Leonowens; a small point admittedly, but typical of how the woman tried to 'massage' her family background for her own social advancement. She even pushed her own son's claim to be the founder of Bangkok's most famous hotel, The Oriental!

In her diaries (upon which *Anna and The King of Siam* – and thus the musical's storyline – would be based), she portrayed the King as an immoral, boorish man and his kingdom as 'barbaric'. As a current official Thai handbook sighs: 'People believed what she wrote and, unfortunately, some still do today!'

Be it noted however that in March 1985, while on a visit to the United States, the current Thai Queen Sirikit took herself and 34 guests (including 20 ladies-in-waiting) to the New York Broadway stage production of *The King and I*. A theatre spokesman said: 'She seemed to enjoy it and did not appear to be offended.'

Afterwards, the Queen visited the cast backstage and told them: 'I enjoyed the play so much. It was wonderful of you to play so beautifully.' To which, the ever-suave Yul Brynner replied: 'We have done so many things about your country without really knowing it. But we do it with great love.'

This encounter between the two may not have led to a 'Shall We Dance' invitation backstage or even to 'Something Wonderful' – but it can certainly be filed under the heading 'Getting to Know You'.

Nor does Father Time heal the wound. In late-1998, 20th Century Fox were remaking *The King and I* movie and naturally wanted to film on location in Thailand. Even though Chow Yun Fatt and Jodie Foster were playing the lead roles and despite the probable big financial spin-offs for Thailand, permission was refused on the grounds of its script 'misinterpreting Thai history'. In other words, it would have Yun Fatt still portraying King Rama IV as a buffoon. So the movie company shifted its location work to Malaysia.

Indeed, during the 1890s, the King made Singapore virtually a second home and usually did so on a 'no-fuss' basis. His frequent visits proved significant for his kingdom, for Singapore served as a conduit for influencing his mind and thus his country towards more modern ways. Such as by introducing railways, telephones, electric lights, hospitals – and the English language. The King would send 20 of his sons and nephews for an education at Singapore's Raffles Institution, three of whom went on to England to complete their studies.

An Astute Investment in Orchard Road

The King also made what was to prove an astute purchase of some land just off the north end of what was then quiet, rural Orchard Road.

First he bought Hurricane House, erstwhile home of Captain William Scott (who had been both Harbour Master and Post Master of Singapore). Hurricane House and its immediate grounds stood pretty much on the area now covered by the Marriott Hotel and Scotts Shopping Centre. Then in 1897, he spent $7,000 on more land from Scott's old plantation grounds (the Claymore Estate).

This has since shrunk but Thailand still owns a sizeable 18,386 sq metre site, on which stands the Royal Thai Embassy – known to many Singaporeans as *Durians* the site of regular outdoor Thai Fruit Fairs which *galore ...* sell massive Thai durians along with mangos, mangosteens and the like. This freehold land is about the last 'under-exploited' plot anywhere along Orchard Road, and Thai officials are keenly aware of how much it could reap from King Rama V's Singapore purchase.

His initial visit to Singapore sparked off a personal lifelong interest in travel; he twice visited Europe around the turn of the century and, reportedly, 'charmed people wherever he went'. King Rama V also had a great interest in cooking, coming up with a cookbook adapting European recipes inspired by his travels there. He died in 1910, his country by then well along its path to modernisation. Many Thais still regard his 42-year reign as 'The Golden Age of Siam'.

The Siamese King's elephant arrived here the year after that 1871 first visit as a token of his gratitude. It went up on 25 June in front of what was the Town Hall (now the Victoria Concert Hall and Theatre).

It was moved to its current Parliament House site in 1919 during the reorganisations the Singapore centenary celebrations required. Its pedestal has inscriptions in four languages – Thai, Jawi, Chinese and English, all spelling out that 'first visit by Siamese monarch' message.

The elephant survived the 1942–45 Occupation intact, for the Japanese regarded Siam as a neutral country. The sweet

From Siam to Thailand

The ancient kingdom of Siam changed its name to the present Thailand (meaning 'Land of the Free') in May 1949.

little thing is black and was meant to be black, but has turned green and red in its time through the mischievous paintbrushes of pranksters. Pink, too: this happened in the 1930s when sporting European humidity-hit members of the nearby Singapore Cricket Club broke a long sequence of rugby and cricket defeats at the hands of local teams. Their celebrations took the form of painting the town red – and the elephant pink.

The black-again elephant is still there outside Parliament House to remind us of this progressive and affable monarch. But in the interests of Asean goodwill, it should be pointed out that after his first visit to Singapore, the King went on to Jakarta and later presented that city with a similar whimsical little black elephant, which today stands outside Jakarta's National Museum.

That Man Raffles

The Stamford Raffles statues
Empress Place and Boat Quay

Stamford Raffles founded more than just
Singapore – he also 'rediscovered' Borobudur ...

W hen the first Stamford Raffles statue – the one now
outside the Victoria Memorial Hall – was formally
unveiled on 27 June 1887 during the Jubilee Year of Queen
Victoria, an audible gasp arose from sections of the assembled
throng. A translation came back to shock the
officiating party. Malays in the crowd had **Gasp! Was**
excitedly remarked: 'Aiyah! Dia orang hitam **Raffles black**
macam kita!' Or: 'Wah! He was a black man like
us!'

No doubt the governor in charge of the ceremony, Sir
Frederick Weld, acted quickly to dispel this rumour by assuring
all of Sir Stamford's Caucasian pigmentation. It was just the
statue that was black, that was just the way these sculptor
wallahs did things, it didn't mean Raffles was actually a black
man, etc.

This statue was then placed on the Padang at the St
Andrew's Cathedral end. In February 1919, the month of the
Singapore centenary, the statue was shifted to its current site
– which, interestingly, was the same location for an equally
large crowd who had gathered in February 1963 to watch
television make its debut here in the form of a 15-minute film
called *TV Looks at Singapore*. Some 500 people watched this very
first RTS programme on 17 black-and-white TV sets arranged
outside the Victoria Memorial Hall.

At the February 1919 ceremony, a verbose tribute was
delivered on behalf of the Chinese Chamber of Commerce.
Here be extracts: 'We, the descendants of a great and ancient
people, in consequence of his (i.e. Raffles's) broad-minded and

remarkable foresight, have been enabled to seek our fortunes and obtain a livelihood here in peace and security. Let us hope that our descendants, a hundred years hence, will have equal cause with us today for congratulation upon the great progress which marks the passing of our first centenary.'

To which Governor Sir Arthur Young responded with a tribute to Singapore's Chinese: '... on the arrival of Sir Stamford 100 years ago, there was no Chinese community – now, in this port of 300,000 inhabitants, there are over 200,000 Chinese ... I have learnt to admire the Chinese for their energy and independence, and for their invariable kindness and readiness in coming to the assistance of their poorer brethren.' Fulsome stuff, but take note: some historians insist there was already a handful of Chinese here (as gambier planters) before Raffles arrived in February 1819.

Transferring the Raffles statue in 1919 to its current site meant displacing the King of Siam's elephant, which in its turn was moved to outside Parliament House. The Raffles statue then had a charming little Italian-style colonnade behind it but this came to grief during the pre-invasion Japanese air-bombings, with the statue itself suffering only minor damage.

Surviving the Japanese Occupation

Major damage was nearly its fate when the Japanese marched in. The statue was taken down and sent to the National Museum while its future was decided. Some Japanese argued that it should be melted down for its copper content, some said it should go to a planned Tokyo museum of imperial conquests. Marquis Tokugawa, the museum's new Japanese curator, instead hid the statue in a basement storeroom, for he was a man with a feel for history. Having a feel also for his neck, he reported it destroyed. The statue re-emerged unscathed at war's end.

Up it went again on 6 July 1946, the day after the anniversary of Raffles's birth/death. Yes, he was one of those few people who died on their birthdays; in Raffles's case, recent

Was Raffles a Playboy?

Stamford Raffles may well have slept on the same pillow (as the charmingly-opaque Malay phrase has it) as women who were not his wife. It has been claimed that a distinctive 170-year-old grave by itself on the pavement along Stevens Road is the final resting place of Raffles's Chinese mistress. Here lies Chen Cui Yun who was rather rich and who, according to a reported remark from an old man interrupted while visiting the grave in the belief that she was an ancestor, was 'the mistress of a big, important man'. Who knows?

evidence suggests, from the crippling effects of tertiary syphilis (the Aids of this pre-penicillin era). More dignified history books record Raffles's death as due to a brain haemorrhage which caused him to tumble down the stairs of his home at Hendon in north London, and die soon afterwards.

Another Close Shave

The Raffles statue came under threat again in 1959 when the People's Action Party (PAP), on a high tide of anti-colonial feeling, came close to destroying it. Former Foreign Minister Mr S. Rajaratnam explained how close: 'He escaped by a narrow margin. Now we have polished him up. He has an honourable place. To pretend that he did not found Singapore is the first sign of a dishonest society.' The polish-up, incidentally, was necessary as the 'black' man was turning green through exposure to the elements.

The 'greening' of Raffles ...

The PAP's sophisticated treatment of the Raffles statue did not go unnoticed by outsiders. As Prime Minister Mr Lee Kuan Yew explained when he came in December 1970 to deliver a Visitor's Dinner Speech at the Singapore Cricket Club, just across the road from the statue.

He quoted words spoken to him earlier that year by Dr Albert Winsemius, the Dutch economic boffin and distinguished ex-United Nations figure, who had been coming to Singapore on and off since 1960 with advice on how the country could get rich. Mr Lee said he had asked the boffin when he thought was making Singapore so obviously succeed in becoming so. Part of his answer was: 'You have the statue of Stamford Raffles still out there.'

Pressed by a curious Prime Minister as to the deeper significance of this remark, Dr Winsemius explained: 'There are not many places in the world where they give credit to the man who founded it.' Warming to his theme, he went on: 'When you tear down what has been built up and you

Indian National Army

In 1998, a National Heritage Board memorial was erected just off the Padang to recognise a remarkable event here in July 1945. Then, just months before the Japanese surrender, the foundation stone was laid for a memorial to commemorate the Indian National Army's 'unknown soldier'. This event was presided over by INA leader Subhas Chandra Bose, while the stone was engraved with the Urdu words for unity, faith and sacrifice.

This memorial was quickly destroyed when the British returned, as it was within direct sight of the City Hall steps where Lord Mountbatten received Japan's formal surrender of Singapore. The INA was formed in 1942 (with Japanese support) with the aim of liberating India from the British and with the keynote chant 'To Delhi! To Delhi!' It was made up mainly of Japanese PoWs from the British Indian Army but achieved little military success. Bose himself disappeared in mysterious circumstances shortly after that INA ceremony on the Padang.

symbolically bury the people who built up the place, then you are in for a lot of trouble. When people see this (statue), they think "This place must be reasonable and sane. It has not been stricken by madness".' He meant this to refer also to the Padang itself, in the sense of leaving such a large grassy space open to all and untouched, in the very heart of town.

It is true that with the coming of its statehood, Singapore did not rush about – like many, many other post-colonial countries in their first hot flush of independence – destroying its colonial tokens and changing all its street names, etc. As Devan Nair, Singapore's third President (from October 1981 till, abruptly, March 1985) put it: 'We are probably unique in the Commonwealth in that we have never been guilty of xenophobia in dealing with our British past.' Ireland, for instance, renamed its Queenstown as Cobh when Britain left.

Much the same point was made in a June 1994 magazine interview by Professor Tommy Koh, the National Arts Council chairman. He said: 'Singapore has no colonial hangover and hence, we are fortunately not saddled with narrow parochialism and strong nationalism. Singapore harbours no such prejudices.'

London in Singapore

Indeed, most significant British colonialists are still noted by street names. Plus there's that pleasing surprise for those acquainted with London, if they visit a cluster of streets just south of Seletar airport and near Seletar Country Club. There, they'll find the likes of Oxford Street, Park Lane, Piccadilly Circus, Regent Street, Knightsbridge, Battersea Road, Lambeth Walk, The Oval, Maida Vale and such like (even Mornington Crescent), dating from the area's previous British air force occupancy.

And so it is that the Raffles statue still attracts the shutterbugs, while Raffles himself gazes in mute frozen concentration at the soaring towers of Mammon just across the Singapore river from his own colonial quarter. On his pedestal is his family coat of arms, while dug deep beneath him (in 1919) is a time capsule bottle with dull things like newspapers and coins.

There is, of course, another Raffles statue: this one in white polymarble, made from plaster casts of the original Raffles and standing on Boat Quay behind Parliament House, alongside the river walk. This marks the official Raffles Landing Site, that is, the precise spot at which Raffles first stepped ashore, that day in February 1819. Or did he?

So where exactly did Raffles land?

The site can only be a guess, at best. There are some who argue that the Raffles party in fact rowed up the Rochor river, meaning the man stepped ashore close to that river's curve under today's Crawford Bridge.

Indeed, the only agreed aspects of Raffles's arrival is that the first food he sampled upon Singaporean soil were the rambutans from among the various fruits offered in greeting to him by hospitable Malays and that there were probably about 1,000 people living here (mainly along the Kallang and Seletar rivers) when Raffles arrived.

Whatever the case, the second Raffles statue marks the spot – and that's official. This statue is the responsibility of the Singapore Tourism Board, which takes its duties seriously as it regularly has to patch up unfortunate-looking stains on this Raffles, caused by its polymarble's problems with the local humidity. The pedestal upon which this Raffles stands records the official version of his landing.

Rediscovered: Borobudur

Stamford Raffles nearly didn't see the birth of modern Singapore – 'a child of my own', as he tagged it. In 1816, he was recalled to London from his post as Lt Governor General in Batavia (now Jakarta) on Java, which was then under British dictate as its previous colonial master, the Netherlands, had been 'acquired' by Britain's great imperial enemy, Napoleon's France.

It is testimony to Raffles's feel for Southeast Asia that before leaving Java, he ordered officials to 'rediscover' the Borobudur temple he'd read about near Yogyakarta in Central Java, and then hidden under volcanic soil, jungle and all sorts. Raffles had started the process whereby Indonesia can now proudly offer to the world the magnificently-restored Borobudur as its 'legacy to mankind'.

But in 1816, the Dutch East Indies (today's Indonesia) was to be returned to Dutch control (Napoleon's power had been smashed at the 1815 Battle of Waterloo). And Raffles was out of a job, heading for a London desk-bound post with Britain's East India Company.

Preserved for Prosperity

When he finally died on St Helena, various Napoleon body parts were 'pickled' – including his penis. Napoleon's sexual prowess had been legendary but at his postmortem, a doctor recorded how small, even 'underdeveloped', his sexual organs were.

Napoleon's penis now swims in a jar of formaldehyde in a New York hospital. Dr John Lattimer, an American urologist, bought the 'item' at a Christie's London 1972 auction for US$4,000. He described it as looking 'like a small, shrivelled finger'. He added: 'But it has been sitting in the jar for a very long time.'

Raffles: A man with a mission.

On his way back, after rounding Cape Town and putting in at the isolated British island of St Helena for supplies, Raffles seized the chance to confront the era's superstar, the man who had forced Raffles to so reluctantly quit Southeast Asia – Napoleon himself, exiled to this tiny speck on the world map where after six pointless years he was to die of a gastric ulcer (or poisoned, as some French people still insist).

In a postcard back to Penang, Raffles recorded: 'Now behold me in the presence of the greatest man of the age!' But in reality, Raffles was subjected to a 10-minute monologue during which, among other things, Napoleon demanded to know what the Java coffee he was never to know tasted like and whether Batavia was as 'unhealthy' as he had heard. Then, Napoleon snubbed Raffles by just walking off, lost in his own mental world. Raffles's final description of the 'greatest man of the age'? He recorded, ungenerously: 'The man is a monster ...'

Napoleon a monster?

Singapore has two Raffles statues, as well as numerous roads, buildings, hotels, schools, cocktails, monkeys (the cheeky long-tailed macaques on Sentosa), flowers (the Rafflesia) and more named after him (though none have used his middle name of Bingley). He has his memorials in London, too. At the north Hendon church (still villagey in feel and worth a visit), at the London Zoo which he co-founded (a bust of his face sits in the Lion's House) – and most dignified of all, in the celebration of all Britain's great that is Westminster Abbey.

Raffles's statue stands in the northern aisle of the Abbey's nave, with a long inscription recording the man's many achievements. Including setting up 'an emporium at Singapore'. An emporium?!

A True War Hero

Lim Bo Seng Memorial
Connaught Drive

'Without such courageous men, wars are not
won nor is independent freedom gained.'

This is the single most striking memorial along the
Esplanade. For a start, it is clearly no token of the British
colonialist presence in Singapore. It's a 3.6-m high Chinese
pagoda (sculpted by Robert Ng) with a bronze top and white
marble cladding, all 'guarded' by four bronze lions.

It's Singapore's public commemoration of Lim Bo Seng, the
most notable among those local Chinese who opposed the
'replacement' colonial presence of Japan. The memorial was
unveiled on 29 June 1954, exactly ten years after his death at
the hands of the Japanese Kempeitai (secret police). Bo Seng
has another lasting memorial in Singapore: his physical remains
lie buried at a graceful spot alongside the MacRitchie Reservoir,
near the main entrance on Lornie Road.

Lim Bo Seng was born in China's Fujian province in 1909.
Though the eleventh born of the 27 children initiated by his
father Lim Chee Gee (who was rich enough to secure the
cooperation of six wives), Bo Seng was Number One Son. So
his future was intended to be spent running his father's thriving
Singapore brick-building and contracting firm (which had
worked on such prominent local landmarks as the Goodwood
Park Hotel and the Victoria Memorial Hall).

A Raffles Institution Boy

Bo Seng first came to Singapore as a 16-year-old to study at
Raffles Institution (a classmate was Yusof bin Ishak, who
became Singapore's first President). He then went to Hong
Kong University but halfway through his studies, his father

*The Lim Bo Seng Memorial – commemorating a martyr
to the cause of a liberated Malaya.*

died and Bo Seng came back to Singapore. He took over family responsibilities and the family business (which, by this stage, was on a downhill slide).

Bo Seng rationalised the firm by concentrating on two brickworks and its noted biscuit factory. Before long, the 'Hock Ann' biscuit brandname regained its reputation. Bo Seng saw to it that his affluence extended to his large family and other dependants.

Bo Seng's initial involvement with the British armed forces came through his firm's contract for the many local defence works required during the 1930s as the reality of the Japanese menace to the region became apparent.

Then in 1937 came the Marco Polo Bridge Incident and Japan's subsequent invasion of China's heartland, giving the Chinese of Singapore a real jolt. This turning-point incident took place on July 7, when a Japanese soldier based by the bridge north of Beijing left his post to urinate. His superiors insisted he was 'abducted' by a nearby Chinese garrison, and Japanese shells soon starting flying at this unit. Japan used this 'incident' as its pretext for launching an all-out attack on China.

Back in Singapore during the 1930s, the China Relief Fund was the main vehicle for funnelling money to China's anti-Japan resistance (though technically, it was supposed to be for 'relief' purposes). It is said that millions of dollars were collected in Singapore for this purpose, both through voluntary donations from the public and through secret levies taken at various Chinese society and association functions.

Lim Bo Seng was jolted more than most by the Marco Polo Bridge Incident. Soon, under the alias Tan Choon Lim, he was playing a leading role in the China Relief Fund and more. It proved mildly ironic that Bo Seng, the rich and ruthless businessman, was to travel up to Kuala Dungun on the Terengganu coast to organise an all-out strike among the workers at a Japanese-owned iron smelting works.

In Singapore itself, Bo Seng was equally active in anti-Japanese activities. So active, in fact, that the British-run Singapore CID issued him with an official pistol and used his services to probe underground Japanese activities on the island.

Following the December 1941 Japanese invasion of Malaya at Kota Bharu, Bo Seng organised the 10,000-strong Labour Services emergency work all over the island during those last frantic weeks before the Occupation. His men helped out in the flamboyant (if militarily ineffective) gesture of 'pulling up the drawbridge' – dynamiting the Causeway link from Johor.

Topping the 'Most Wanted' List

It was clear that Bo Seng would be high on any 'mopping-up' list when the Japanese triumphed. Thus he received permission to escape Singapore on one of the few available boats. He had a tearful parting from his wife and seven children at his Telok Ayer Street office. He later noted in his diary: 'The children were too stupified to realise what was happening. Each of them in turn kissed me goodbye. I shall never forget their tear-stained faces as long as I live.'

Bo Seng then sailed away with seven others from Collyer Quay on February 11, just days before the final collapse. He was never to see Singapore again as a live man.

His wife and children went into hiding on St John's island, south of Singapore. A wise precaution. For, the day after the British surrender, Bo Seng's family compound in Upper Serangoon was surrounded by Japanese soldiers. With no Bo Seng in sight, 15 adults living there were taken away. Just eight returned. They were English-educated. Seven were never seen again. They were the Chinese-educated ones.

Bo Seng meanwhile had made his way to China where he joined the nationalist government forces, and was given the job of recruiting for the war effort among the 4,000 Chinese sailors stranded in Calcutta.

While in India, Bo Seng was approached by a group of British Army officers planning a guerilla counterattack in the Malayan jungles. They wanted Bo Seng to join them with a specially-trained group of Chinese guerillas. Approval came from nationalist China, Bo Seng was given the title of Lt-Col and he prepared himself and his men for their jungle-fighting role in what was called Force 136.

The majority of his Chinese guerillas were at least in sympathy with communism, if not out-and-out party members. The political sympathies of Bo Seng (by now using the alias Tan Choon Lim) scarcely lay in that direction. It was the conditions of war and the unity of intent in opposing the Japanese that threw up such unlikely – and strictly temporary – political alliances.

Return to Malaya

Bo Seng and his men reached Malaya by submarine in November 1943. Just four months later, while in Ipoh to gather supplies and information on enemy troop movements, Bo Seng was identified by a spy and arrested by the Japanese. He was taken to the prison at Batu Gajah, just south of Ipoh and his agony began. He was tortured round the clock, as Kempeitai officers strove to extract from him the names of his fellow guerillas and details of the full extent of anti-Japanese guerilla activities.

For three agonising months, Bo Seng held out. Only death could provide release. This came on 29 June 1944 when, as a respectful British officer put it, Bo Seng 'died

Three agonising months ...

with his lips sealed'. He was buried in a shallow grave behind the prison. He was 35 years old.

After the Japanese surrender, the Chinese government honoured him with the posthumous title of Major-General, while the British government gave his widow an annual pension of 400 pounds. Bo Seng's remains were brought back to Singapore where he was honoured with a moving memorial service on the steps of City Hall on 13 January 1946. Then, flanked by armoured cars and guards of honour from British and Chinese troops (mainly survivors of Force 136), Bo Seng was taken for state burial at MacRitchie Reservoir.

Justice for Bo Seng

Bo Seng's tormentors did not escape, though they came close. Sub-Lt Yamaguchi and Sgt-Major Shimomura were the two Kempeitai officers primarily responsible for Bo Seng's 'interrogation'. They were held at Changi prison after the surrender while awaiting trial – until the British military authorities began an information hunt on Malayan Communist

Party activities. All temporary political wartime bets were suddenly off. The enemy was now communism.

A new enemy ...

And the two Japanese secret service men in Changi were experts on the local communist party. So, they were released and debriefed. Their information proved so useful, a deal was almost struck that would allow their quick (and quiet) return to Japan. But Bo Seng's remains had only just been returned to Singapore. And the public's mood was not a 'forgive and forget' one.

So Yamaguchi and Shimomura were duly hanged on 19 June 1946. Their final utterance as they mounted the 13 steps to the Changi scaffold was the traditional 'Banzai!', or 'Long live the Emperor!'

When the Lim Bo Seng Memorial's foundation stone was laid in 1953 by Malcolm MacDonald, then British Commissioner-General for Southeast Asia, he said of the war hero: 'He died so that Singapore and Malaya might be the home of free people who could enjoy once again peace, prosperity and happiness.'

An inscription on the memorial (which cost some $50,000, money raised in large part from the public) states that Lim Bo Seng died a 'martyr to the cause of a liberated Malaya and to his loyalty to his comrades'. The account it carries of his life is inscribed in the nation's four official languages – English, Chinese, Malay and Tamil.

Bo Seng's Diary

When the National Museum staged its vivid 'When Singapore was Syonan-To' exhibition in February 1992 (to mark the 50th anniversary of the British surrender), one of its prize displays was Lim Bo Seng's diary. This was the first time it had been seen in public.

The diary had been given, post-war, by the British to Bo Seng's wife – from whom it had passed onto Mr Lim Leong Geok, Bo Seng's son. Leong Geok was just 10 years old when he last saw his father alive in that Telok Ayer Street office.

A Lasting Message

Mrs Lim Bo Seng died on 25 September 1979. Her husband had left her a message in his diary, just before leaving Calcutta for Malaya. It was as if he knew he would never see her again: 'You must not grieve for me. On the other hand, you should take pride in my sacrifice.'

She did. Her words, after her husband's state burial, were memorable: 'It's all part of war. I harbour no hatred. After all, hatred can only bring misery to the world.'

The Esplanade memorial is still honoured every year with small wreaths of flowers left there by Lim family members, veteran Caucasian fellow members of Force 136 and others. One recent year, a wreath carried this message: 'Without such courageous men, wars are not won nor is independent freedom gained.'

On 29 June 1994 (the 50th anniversary of Bo Seng's death), a special ceremony was held at his memorial, with Minister for Information and the Arts BG George Yeo laying a wreath and paying warm tribute to Bo Seng and his fellow fighters in

Elizabeth Choy

Sabah-born Elizabeth Choy is Singapore's authentic female war hero. In 1943, she and her husband helped run an illicit in-and-out information service for PoWs held by the Japanese in a Woodbridge hospital camp. For this, the couple were themselves arrested. Mrs Choy was held for 200 days at the secret police's YMCA HQ where her torture included endless electrical shocks and being forced to drink her own urine.

After the war, Mrs Choy and her husband were awarded with OBEs by the British and she went on to become the first woman nominated (in 1951) to the Legislative Council, Singapore's pre-independence decision-making body. In 1973, Mrs Choy was awarded the Pingat Bakti Setia (long-service medal) by the Singapore government. In 1997, she published her autobiography, from which we learnt that she was (in 1949) the artist's nude model for a lovely sculpture called Serene Jade which has been displayed at the National Museum.

Force 136. One young attendee at the memorial, 17-year-old student Mohammad Fayzal, said of Bo Seng: 'There are not many heroes in Singapore, but he is definitely one of them.'

They Will Not Be Forgotten

Memorial to the Civilian Victims of
the Japanese Occupation
junction of Beach and Bras Basah roads

*Tens of thousands of civilians were killed
during World War II, many of them victims of
the Operation Sweep-Up massacres ...*

The four tapered 67.4-m high columns of this war memorial surge towards the sky, symbolically coming close together at the top. Known (affectionately) as the 'chopsticks' monument, it was unveiled by then Prime Minister Mr Lee Kuan Yew on 15 February 1967 – 25 years to the day after Britain surrendered to the Japanese.

The memorial commemorates the 'civilian victims of the Japanese Occupation'. Within it, an urn containing the ashes of some of those dead civilians stands on a pedestal, which carries these words: 'In deep and lasting sorrow, this memorial is dedicated in memory of those of our civilians who were killed between 15 February 1942 and 16 August 1945 when the Japanese Armed Forces occupied Singapore.' In the ground below the memorial lie the remains of many more of those civilians.

They died in the daily bombing raids that started early on the morning of 8 December 1941 as Japanese air attacks 'softened up' the island in readiness for a land attack. They died during the fighting, they died in detention, they died from malnutrition and illness during the Occupation. They died, most of all, in the three weeks after the surrender during Operation Sweep-Up, or Sook Ching in Chinese.

Just how many did die? Japanese estimates given during war crime trials put the figure at 6,000 dead after 'interrogation' and 9,000 dead as civilian war casualties. The true figure is more like 30,000 dead, though it will for ever remain impossible to get an exact figure. At his war crimes trial, Col Sugita (the intelligence chief wrongly assumed to have masterminded

*Surviving family members remember a victim of the
Occupation at the memorial.*

Sweep-Up) allegedly confided to a Japanese journalist that
the order had been to eliminate 50,000 of Singapore's Chinese,
and that almost half this number had been killed.

Victory and Revenge

On 16 February 1942, the day after the surrender, the Japanese
military leadership installed itself in what, just 24 hours before,
had been the British military command base – Fort Canning
Hill's underground bunker. Immediate revenge against
Singapore's Chinese was high on the Japanese agenda.

The last straw for Yamashita had been the dogged resistance
his troops encountered at the hands of the Civil Defence forces,
the Singapore Chinese Volunteer Company and 'Dalforce', an

emergency band of irregulars formed largely from convicted violent Chinese criminals serving long sentences in Changi jail (where they'd been given the 'do or die' option of fighting the Japanese or awaiting an even more uncertain fate).

Do or die ...

Also in Dalforce were China Relief Fund supporters, who after the 1937 Japanese invasion of China felt that money raising and pamphlets alone were not enough. Both groups had personal reasons to fight during the final stages of the Battle for Singapore with a ferocity that did not find an echo with the retreating Allied soldiers (except most notably for the 22nd and 27th Australian Brigades at Kranji and the 1st Battalion Malay Regiment at what is today's Kent Ridge Park).

Besides, the Japanese were anxious to move on to Sumatra and then to Australia, leaving behind just a defence force to hold Singapore. Before this would be possible, went the argument, it was essential to 'sweep up' all those anti-Japanese elements who were not likely to accept the dictates of the new Syonan-To ('Light of the South'), as Singapore had been quickly renamed. In Hokkien dialect, that word Syonan sounded much like 'birdcage'.

So, now that Yamashita had captured Singapore, he indeed vowed to 'sweep away these treacherous Chinese elements'. He ordered: 'Make a thorough job of it.' Yamashita meant it to be a three-day mopping-up operation, directed against probable suspects. Instead, it turned into a two-week operation (17 February – 4 March) and expanded its fatal dragnet to include teenagers, women and even children.

Because, as we now know, of Lt-Col Masanobu Tsuji. He was the senior military intelligence officer who (it has since emerged) actually directed the 'Chinese Solution' here, immediately after being dispatched to Singapore by Tojo.

Secret documents filed at London's Public Records Office showed that the Chinese massacres were perpetuated at the instigation of Tsuji (tagged by a local newspaper as the 'Butcher of Singapore'), whereas Yamashita actually tried to curb Tsuji's 'indisciplines' – only to fall foul of Tsuji's 'hotline' to the top man in Tokyo (and Yamashita's political enemy), Tojo.

'Butcher of Singapore' ...

A Fateful Meeting

On 16 February, a meeting was speedily called in the Fort Canning military bunker to plan the cauterisation of the Chinese community. The next day, an unusual order went out from 25th Army Headquarters.

The whole male Chinese population of Singapore aged between 18 and 50, was to present itself for 'screening' at various assembly points at noon on 21 February. They were to bring food and drink supplies 'for a few days'. 'Severe punishment' would be meted out to those who refused the summons, or who went into hiding.

At first, people asked: What was this 'registration' process about? Was it merely a rough-and-ready census-taking? Or was it something worse, much worse?

Five of the major assembly points were: the open land behind Jalan Besar Stadium; the eastern end of River Valley Road by its junction with Clemenceau Avenue; an open area near the Tanjong Pagar police station; a rubber factory near the junction of Kallang and Geylang roads; and the open land off Paya Lebar Road (where a fierce battle had been fought just two weeks before).

For some people, there were only hours to wait; for others, up to a week. Closely packed together, without shade and without toilet or washing facilities, Chinese men awaited their 'registration'. One description of the Jalan Besar camp was that its seething concentration of humanity looked like 'settling locusts or hiving bees'.

The lucky ones were given an 'examined' stamp on a piece of paper though under the strain of dealing with so many

An Evil Man

In his 1992 book *The Killer They Called A God*, military historian Ian Ward described how Tsuji – despite being personally responsible for the 'elimination' of tens of thousands of people in Singapore, Malaya and the Philippines – got away with it, through protection by the post-war US which struck a 'plea-bargaining' deal with him.

Tsuji then even went on to become a member of Japan's ruling Liberal Democratic government. Tsuji 'disappeared' during a secret mission to Laos in 1961 and was officially declared dead in 1968. Ward called him: 'The most insidious, calculating, coldly brutal and singularly successful mass killer in the entire Japanese war criminal line-up.'

people, the Japanese soon resorted to simply stamping the clothes the men were wearing. Or even their arms or foreheads, leaving a mark many civilians were reluctant to wash off.

The unlucky ones were those deemed to fall into the following 'undesirable' categories: those with proven China Relief Fund links; all natives of Hainan island – considered by Japanese to be communists; those who could write their names in English but not in Chinese; people who had left China within the previous five years since Japan's military invasion and were thereby suspected of being 'anti-Japanese'; journalists, teachers and high school students; men with tattoo marks who were assumed to be secret society members and thus well out of order.

There was another special assembly zone in Chinatown (now covered by Hong Lim complex). This saw people herded together on the side streets off South Bridge Road – like Mosque, Pagoda and Temple streets – while they awaited registration at the building on the corner of Upper Cross Street and South Bridge Road. Those who 'passed' carried straight on down Upper Cross Street towards Collyer Quay. Those who didn't were made to take a left turn towards waiting lorries.

Families could not get precise information on those who failed to return home after their screening. At first, it was assumed they had been taken away on those lorries to join work parties, either in Singapore or in other places now ruled by the Japanese.

But soon, reports were circulating of bullet-riddled bodies (with their hands tied together behind their backs) turning up at coastal points sweeping a wide arc from *Bullet-riddled bodies ...*
Keppel Harbour around, anticlockwise, to Punggol. One rumour even swept Upper Serangoon that pigs had been seen chewing parts of human bodies nosed up from shallow pits in the Punggol swamps. Chinese in the area abstained for a while from eating pork.

The Carnage

What had really happened to those who 'failed' their screening makes grim reading. Some were taken to Kempeitai centres, particularly its YMCA headquarters. Here, they underwent

Shook Ching Memorial

In 1998, the National Heritage Board marked six new historic war memorial sites, including one for the Sook Ching Centre located on the Hong Lim corner formed by Cross Street and North Bridge Road. Similarly marked were three beach sites where thousands of Chinese civilians were killed by Japanese secret police, following the 1942 Sook Ching screenings – at Changi, Punggol and Sentosa.

water and fire tortures for days on end. But the vast majority of those led away on the back of lorries were coldly shot dead (or beheaded). Mainly at Changi's beach, Punggol, and offshore facing the island we now call Sentosa. At these points, the seawater was said to be turning crimson with human blood.

Historian Ian Ward tracked down one British soldier who, while in wartime hiding on Sentosa, had been a witness to Operation Sweep-Up. Joseph Cusselle, then 74, said: 'Just off the Singapore coast, we could see packages being thrown into the sea from tugs and then being fired on by machine guns. This went on from February 21, 1942.'

When he opened up one of those 'packages' that had washed ashore on Sentosa, he found it contained the body of a young Chinese man. Cusselle was able to show Ward where on Sentosa he'd buried more than 40 of such bullet-riddled corpses that had been washed ashore.

A Great Escape

One nimble-witted young Chinese man in his early 20s had a lucky escape. Rounded up and herded into the back of a lorry for 'removal', he sensed the danger and was able to bluff his guards into letting him return to the collection centre, allegedly to retrieve some belongings. The Japanese pretence was still that those in the lorry were being sent only into forced labour, so he was allowed off. He then made a nippy escape from a near-certain death. The young man's name? Lee Kuan Yew ...

His son Deputy Prime Minister Lee Hsien Loong said in a Japanese newspaper interview in August 1994: 'My mother's brother was taken away by Japanese soldiers and never returned. My father was very nearly taken away at a detention centre. If events had turned out slightly different, I might never have been born.'

Through Japanese Eyes

In May 1994, a controversial limited-edition Japanese book which included eyewitness accounts of Singaporean Chinese massacres was translated into English. It was written by 82-year-old newspaper retiree Mr Naoji Matsumoto (who had been a reporter attached to the wartime Japanese army press corps) for this reason: 'The Japanese people are ignorant of what happened during the Pacific War. So I wanted to tell people what the Japanese military actually did. Our reports from the front were censored, so we could not write the truth then.'

Mr Matsumoto described a 'showpiece' 1942 Sweep-Up execution when he and other Japanese reporters were brought to an area surrounded by wire netting and in which a trench had been dug (he did not specify the exact Singapore location):

'In front of the trench, about 200 people were seated shackled in a row with their hands tied behind their backs. One by one, they were blindfolded. Some tried to resist, shaking their heads. The samurai sword was swung up high into the air. When each head was cut off, blood spurted out and the body fell into the trench.

'After seeing about ten people cut down in this fashion, I became nauseous ...'

And an Australian ex-intelligence officer, Stan Smith, held captive near Changi told Ward: 'We saw many bodies floating in the sea. There were women and youngsters among them ...'

Thousands and thousands were slaughtered in those savage two weeks. Only a handful escaped to provide posterity with written accounts. Mr Cheng Kuan Yew, a civil servant, 'failed' his screening at the Jalan Besar registration centre. With his fellow 'criminals', he was marched to the Victoria School grounds off Kitchener Road and made to squat there for two hours. A fleet of military trucks then appeared.

A survivor's account ...

Detainees had their hands tied behind their backs with thin Manila rope and were herded onto the trucks. This particular 'shipment' had some 400 people, who all assumed they were being taken to make up a work party. When Changi Prison loomed into view, they then thought they were heading for imprisonment. But the trucks continued on – to near the beach.

The men were ordered out and in groups of ten were tied together with telephone wire. They were told to move towards the water's edge. Then, suddenly, machine-gunning started. Mr Cheng was hit and dragged down onto the sand by the falling bodies of the men to whom he was tied. He lay there, very still indeed, as a Japanese soldier stood on his back to bayonet the man next to him. Mr Cheng escaped again as bayonets plunged into the bodies of any of the 400 or so condemned men who were found to be still twitching. He kept his eyes shut tight till he heard the sound of the trucks driving away. Night had just fallen.

He eased free of his bindings, saw that many men were still just about alive, heard their agonised cries as they lay bound and bleeding on Changi beach. Terrified, he managed to get clear and have his wounds tended at Raffles Institution in town (then being used as a military hospital). The memory of that chilling afternoon on the beach was not so easily treated.

The beach executions continued for days, turning the sand red. Some men tried to escape after getting off the lorries as soon as they realised what was about to happen. They fled away back inland, pursued by Japanese machine gun bullets. Some did escape and 'disappeared' back into their communities. Other Sweep-Up executions took the form of making doomed groups dig a long trench, then making them kneel alongside it. They were then bayoneted in the backs, one by one, and pushed forward into the mass grave they'd just dug.

Back in town, it was reported that a 22-strong Chinese family unit was massacred in their now-demolished house at Muhammed Ali Lane, running between South Bridge Road and Cross Street.

The full extent of these killings was not realised until after the Japanese surrender. So many people had simply not returned home. But they hadn't been on work parties – in or out of Singapore. They were dead. Post-war, mass graves kept being discovered and the full horror became apparent.

The full horror emerges ...

There was mounting disbelief within the Chinese community. How and why could so many thousands of people have 'disappeared' like that?

War Crime Trials Fiasco

The seething anger was temporarily soothed by the war crime trials of those Japanese officers held responsible for Sweep-Up massacres. These began on 10 March 1947 at the Victoria Memorial Hall, with lawyers for the defence still arguing that the death toll was no higher than 6,000, with 9,000 killed in the actual fighting.

As N.I. Low noted in his book *When Singapore was Syonan-To*: 'In 1942, there were many of us who were pro-Japanese and anti-British. It took the Japanese three years to make us all anti-Japanese. The Kempeitai were mainly responsible for bringing about this change of mind. Thanks to them, we lay under a funereal pall of abject fear. Day and night, awake or asleep, we had them and their devilries in our minds.'

British journalist Dennis Bloodworth, in his book *The Tiger and the Trojan Horse*, accredited a relevant quote to Mr Devan Nair, the anti-colonialist trade unionist who became modern Singapore's third President. In 1941, Mr Nair had told his family: 'Wait till the Japanese arrive. They will treat us like equals, not the way we are being treated by the white man.' It emerged during the Operation Sweep-Up trials at the Victoria Memorial Hall that the 25th Army had placed at its disposal in February 1942 a 'register of anti-Japanese Chinese'. This was a thick book containing personal histories and photographs of 'wanted' Chinese – all prepared by Japanese civilians who had been resident in Singapore during the late 1930s and early 1940s.

The Sweep-Up war crime trials ended on 2 April 1947. As it worked out, they did little to settle Chinese feelings of outrage. Two colonels – Saburo Kawamura and Masyuki Oishi – were condemned to death, and five others to life imprisonment. The British argument was that evidence of individual guilt was inconclusive and that insufficient evidence existed to convict any other Japanese officers. And, as noted, Tsuji – the 'Butcher of Singapore' – got away scot-free.

The impression left on Chinese community leaders, who had worked hard to gather evidence for the trial, was that the British authorities were only really interested in enforcing justice against those Japanese who had committed crimes against the Caucasian community (mainly in connection with the Double Tenth events). And that concern to ensure judicial revenge for the far greater inhumanity against far greater numbers of 'natives' was rather less enthusiastic. All this left another lingering post-Occupation sore that would give momentum to the drive for independence from Britain.

It was also noted that Operation Sweep-Up had been carried out largely by infantry from the 5th Division, which came from the Hiroshima area, and that the beach massacres were carried out largely by the 18th division, which took its members from the Nagasaki area. These two Japanese cities were those which suffered the ferocity of the two US A-bombs in August 1945.

Mass Graves Discovered

The ashes of the Chinese and other civilian victims that lie in the urn inside the chopsticks memorial and the bones buried underneath it can only be symbolic. Most of the thousands who were killed received no kind of burial. Their bodies just disappeared. At sea, in swamps, in mass graves. They are all honoured by this Memorial for the Civilian Victims of the Japanese Occupation.

Wartime Guilt

Japan's wartime guilt is still a sensitive issue with older Singaporeans. This is not helped by Japan's deep and long-lasting reluctance to accept its guilt. For it wasn't until July 1990 that the first unambiguous Japanese statement of official regret was widely publicised. This came from Japanese Foreign Minister Taro Nakayama in Jakarta as he addressed a closed-doors session with Japan's Asean trading partners.

Following this, two Japanese Prime Ministers (Kaifu and Hosokawa) were explicit in publicly acknowledging that wartime Japan had done very wrong. For his pains, Hosokawa was shot at in May 1994 at a Tokyo hotel by a lone right-wing extremist in protest at his 'admission' of Japanese aggression.

Yet even so, the matter still wasn't resolved once and for all. In May 1994, Japan's new Justice Minister Mr Shigeto Nagano (an ex-soldier) insisted that the 1937–38 Rape of Nanking (when up to 200,000 Chinese civilians were massacred by the invading Japanese army) was a 'fabrication'.

All the barely-healed wounds in the region were immediately reopened, and Mr Nagano had to recant and then resign. His Prime Minister, Tsutomu Hata, was forced into a major 'damage limitation' exercise as he assured Japan's Asian wartime conquests (especially China and Korea) that Japan did accept responsibility for waging wars of aggression in the 1930s and '40s. And that the Rape of Nanking (now Nanjing) did actually take place.

And in July and August 1994, Japanese Prime Minister Tomiichi Murayama expressed the most purposeful 'deep remorse' yet for Japan's wartime 'aggression and colonial rule'. He needed to, for in August 1994, yet another Japanese minister – Shin Sakurai (the fourth such in eight years) – was obliged to resign after yet another attempted whitewash job on Japan's wartime record. He had even claimed that Japan's various (13 in all) occupations had 'led to independence, the popularisation of education and increased literacy in Asia'. Good grief!

During 1998, Japanese Prime Minister Keizo Obuchi issued a series of formal written apologies to neighbouring countries, including Korea and China, for Japan's wartime record. Regarded as a bid by Japan to 'clear the slate' of old wounds before the new millennium, the spirit of these apologies was welcomed by SAR Hong Kong's Chief Executive Mr Tung Chee Hwa, who commented: 'We need to learn lessons from the past but also need to bury the past and not be a slave of the past.'

But in November 1998, after the ground-breaking visit to Tokyo by China's President Jiang Zemin, a new frosty impasse was reached when, in Beijing's eyes, Japan refused to offer an adequate written war apology. The precise (translated) wording in the joint communique issued after summit talks between President Jiang and Japanese PM Mr Keizo Obuchi stated that Japan 'is keenly conscious of the responsibility for the serious suffering and damage that Japan inflicted upon the Chinese people through its aggression against China during a certain period in the past and expressed deep remorse for this'. For Beijing, such words still fell short ...

It was erected at the instigation of the Singapore Chinese Chamber of Commerce and Industry, following discovery of a mass grave in January 1962 in the Pasir Puteh area. This led to a wider hunt for unmarked mass graves. Such were found at Siglap, Bedok, Jalan Tiga Ratus, Changi, behind Nanyang Girls' School and elsewhere.

With the discovery of so many graves, the desire – the need – for a permanent memorial intensified. So did some form of official recognition of war guilt from Japan. In the Treaty of San Francisco (aimed at tying up loose ends from the war) which Britain and Japan signed in 1952, there was resentment from Singapore's Chinese that Britain had failed to insist upon a clause being inserted to enforce Japan's atonement.

This resentment mounted and, fired by the continuing discoveries of mass graves, an angry 'Blood Debt' rally was organised by the SCCCI at the Padang on 25 August 1963 to demand a $50 million atonement sum of money from by-then prosperous again Japan. The figure was meant **'Blood debt' rally ...** to evoke the $50 million 'ransom' Gen Yamashita had demanded from the Chinese population of Singapore in 1942.

Large sections of Malaysia's Chinese community took up this call and the figure was raised to $180 million. After intergovernmental negotiations lasting many years, it was finally agreed that Japan hand over $50 million to Singapore – $25 million as a 'gift' and $25 million in the form of a special loan. For Malaysia, two ocean-going ships worth $25 million were presented as a goodwill gesture to settle the 'Blood Debt'.

When Singapore was Syonan-To

When opening the National Museum's 'When Singapore was Syonan-To' exhibition in February 1992, Prime Minister Mr Goh Chok Tong said: 'The 44 months of Japanese Occupation were a period of terror, fear and atrocities. It was also a period of bravery, patriotism and sacrifice.' Mr Goh also noted that four-fifths of Singapore's current population were not even born when Singapore was Syonan-To.

One at the exhibition opening who lived through that era was 67-year-old Mr H.C. Lim, who described the typical day-by-day Occupation meal: 'We ate porridge mixed with tapioca and noodles made of tapioca flour, in which red palm oil was added to make it nutritious. We felt hungry all the time.'

When a 25-year-old engineer saw exhibition photos of Singaporeans beheaded by Japanese troops, his reaction was this: 'The pictures are sickening. I've lost my appetite ...'

War Website

The harsh realities of the 1942–45 Occupation years have now been committed also to virtual reality – with a Battlefield Singapore website at www.s1942.org.sg.

Chopsticks Stand Proud

As for that chopsticks memorial, the SCCCI took four years to raise half the required $500,000, with the government contributing the rest on a dollar-for-dollar basis. A month after its official unveiling, a five-man Japanese team led by Mr Yonosuke Nakano, a veteran pacifist, came to pay its symbolic respect to the dead as a 'mark of atonement'.

Each year on 15 February, a simple memorial service is held at the chopsticks memorial, including a three-minute silence. This is attended mainly by now very old men and women who lost their closest ones during the Occupation, and who cannot forget. A wreath is symbolically placed by representatives of the four major communities in Singapore. And the Japanese ambassador to Singapore pays annual respect.

It is right that the memorial does stand at such a central spot in modern Singapore's Civic and Cultural District. It truly merits respect from the thousands of Singaporeans (and visitors) who pass by it every day, rushing about on their normal business.

For as then Prime Minister (and one-time Operation Sweep-Up escapee) Mr Lee Kuan Yew put it, when arguing to the annual World Economic Forum in 1990 that Europe should balance out Japan's economic influence in Southeast Asia: 'Although memories of the Japan of World War II have been overlaid by better experiences in trade, aid, investments and tourism, the scars have not vanished ...'

Mutinous Daze

The 1915 Sepoy Mutiny
*St Andrew's Cathedral wall plaques,
St Andrew's Road*

*In 1915, an amazing outburst of violence that
eventually left over 40 people dead greeted
Lunar New Year revellers ...*

The 1914 outbreak of World War I in far-off Europe didn't impinge so much on everyday life in Singapore. Certainly the lively German community was soon branded by the British as 'enemy citizens' and stripped of their possessions, their businesses and their Teutonia Club. Some wealthy Chinese citizens donated enough money to buy 53 warplanes to help the far-off British war effort. And during 1915 in Raffles Hotel, the Singapore Sling was invented.

But by and large, life continued as per normal here. Except, that is, for an astonishing outburst of violence that flared up while most people were enjoying the Lunar New Year on 15 February 1915. The Sepoy Mutiny had exploded.

It was to last nearly 10 days, during which time 40 people were shot dead in the streets (including two festive Hokkien Chinese – Sim Soh and Lim Eng Wee – and a Malay chauffeur who shared the same doom as the two Europeans in the back of the car he was driving). When it all ended, 36 sepoys were executed in public by a firing squad. Singapore had been awoken from its slumbers with a savage jolt ...

A Warship Called Emden

The Sepoy Mutiny episode began indirectly with a German warship named Emden. It had sailed south from China and was conducting a solo sea battle in the Indian Ocean, sinking over 20 ships that belonged to the Kaiser's enemies (including a few in Penang harbour) before itself being sunk in November 1914 just off the Cocos Islands by an Australian warship named Sydney.

German survivors were taken to Singapore and imprisoned at the Tanglin military barracks. Their most senior officer was Julius Lauterbach, who soon formed a bond with the Indian soldiers guarding him and his men.

These Indians belonged to the 5th Light Infantry, a regiment whose members were all Punjabi Muslims (800 of them) – about the only full-time British soldiers left in Singapore. Their loyalty was already tested with the news that Muslim Turkey had joined the war on Germany's side against Britain.

The regiment was about to be transferred to Hong Kong when a false rumour spread through their ranks that it was really Turkey to which they were being sent. And there, they would be expected to fight against their co-religionists.

Wild rumours ...

Another wilder rumour even suggested that once they were out at sea, their boat would be sunk by the British as a pre-emptive strike against potential enemies 'from within'.

With this edginess in the air, Herr Lauterbach re-entered the picture. Subsequent inquiries pinpointed him as a key influence on the worried Indian soldiers, advising them to resist the transfer – by force of arms if necessary. He had already provoked his guards by insisting that Indian soldiers were being used as human cannon-fodder by the British on the battlefields of France.

Exceeding this German agitation was the influence of Kassim Mansoor, a Gujarati Muslim, whose coffeeshop was close to the Alexandra barracks off Pasir Panjang Road where the Indian (or 'sepoy') regiment was based. In December 1914, Kassim had written to the Turkish consul in Rangoon, asking him to authorise sending a Turkish warship to Singapore to pick up all available Indian Muslim soldiers and transfer them to the warfront.

Afternoon Raid on Alexandra

At 3 pm on that afternoon of 15 February, the Alexandra barracks magazine store was raided. Sixty thousand rounds of ammunition were stolen. The Sepoy Mutiny was on.

Its first victims were those British soldiers who tried to quell the uprising before it burst out of the barracks. Then 100 or so fired-up mutineers made their way to the Tanglin barracks where they released the Emden's German prisoners and implored them to mastermind a coup d'etat that would take over the whole island of Singapore.

Other mutineers made their way towards Chinatown where they shot dead any British officials or civilians they encountered. Another 100 or so spread around the Pasir Panjang area where one of their victims included a British woman – the only female victim of the rising.

There was a British 'own goal' on Mount Faber at night. Gunner P. Walton of the Singapore Volunteer Artillery failed to reply to a sentry's challenge and was shot dead. The later official inquiry noted: 'It is thought that Mr Walton, who had somnambulist tendencies, was walking in his sleep.'

The freed German prisoners wanted nothing to do with their new friends. The dashing Lauterbach simply used the sudden confusion as a cloak under which he and eight others escaped to Jakarta and eventually back to Berlin. Meanwhile in Singapore, the mutineers asked themselves: 'What shall we do now?' For the harried British authorities were cabling far and wide for emergency troops to rush to the island and help quell the uprising.

The call was answered by French, Japanese and Russian navy men in harbour at the time, plus a 150-strong force led over the Johor Strait, then by train into Tank Road railway station, by a stern and pro-British Sultan Ibrahim. The Sultan personally marched his men from the station and up Fort Canning Hill (declining the offer of an official car for himself), and there awaited further instructions.

His presence helped soothe an early British fear that a 'jihad' (holy war) might develop and spread through the whole of Malaya. Indeed, the only obvious religion-inspired support came from the *imam* of a Kampong Java mosque, who later received a prison sentence for preaching 'sedition' to 5th Light Infantry members.

In the end, only nine mutineers escaped the mopping-up forces. A total of 756 either gave themselves up or were rounded up from various parts of the island. And from Johor, from where the Sultan forcibly returned a 61-strong band who had gone to his *istana* to beg piteously for refuge. Some of their colleagues had even drowned on the way to Johor when desperately swimming across the strait. Fifty-two sepoys died either by drowning or in the fighting.

Court Martials and Executions

The sepoys' next public appearance was at a series of court martials in a South Bridge Road courtroom on 23 February. In all, 85 mutineers were charged, and 42 of them were given the death sentence. In the case of 24 of these, death was later commuted to either transportation to the Andaman Islands for life or imprisonment of up to 20 years. The remaining 43 were also either banished or imprisoned.

Like the trials, the executions (by firing squad) were held as a public warning spectacle. The venue was Outram Prison, built originally by Indian convict labour. Its site is now covered by Outram Park, its shopping centre and its MRT station.

The public of Singapore responded with a ghoulish enthusiasm to the 'entertainment value' of executions in public, with crowds of up to 15,000 flocking to the jail. The condemned men were each tied to a stake in front of the prison wall, with their legs bound and their heads left unhooded – most had bravely refused the offered blindfolds.

The men who were to carry out these judicial killings were members of the Singapore Volunteers – businessmen and civil servants who were *Volunteer* not always skilled marksmen. Inevitably, the *executioners ...* condemned men did not all die immediately. The sight of men writhing in agony while tied to their wooden pillars was not an edifying public spectacle. A British officer went along the row with his revolver, finishing off any not yet dead.

The consequences of the mutiny were many. All Singapore's Indian residents were compelled to register their names, which for most was insulting as they felt their own loyalty was never in doubt. On 8 March, some 3,000 members of the Indian Muslim community held a public meeting, after which a telegram was sent to King George V in London pleading 'the absolute loyalty of all Mohammedans in the colony, a loyalty which never changed and never would change.'

Kassim Mansoor was hanged. He had never realised that his mail to Rangoon was being intercepted by the British censor. He also didn't realise that the Turkish consul had been withdrawn from Rangoon as soon as war was declared in 1914. Convicted of 'waging war against the King', he went to the gallows on 31 May.

British imperial complacency had been severely jolted. The Singapore Volunteers were taken with a new seriousness in the realisation that enemies could come from within the island as much as from outside.

The remaining 'loyal' members of the 5th Light Infantry were sent to western Africa to fight against Germans in the Cameroons. Five years later, the 5th Light was disbanded in a reorganisation of the Indian Army, at which stage it faded from military history.

Calm Amidst the Mutiny

Yet did Singapore really come close to the brink? Did anything really happen to threaten the island's serenity – or even to disrupt the festivities of the 1915 Lunar New Year, the noisy firecrackers of which had largely drowned out the sound of the mutineers' gunfire?

An official report noted: 'The native population was quiet throughout. The Chinese, Malays and Tamils pursued their ordinary vocations as though nothing unusual were occurring. No crowds collected and so far from there being any panic, there was among the Chinese in particular all through the town and country districts an imperturbability which amounted to unconcern. Any feeling that was shown was that of sympathy with the Government. The natives of Northern India showed no sign of any sympathy with the mutineers.'

Even the hapless mutineers themselves were dismissed as misguided stooges. Roland Braddell (whose family gave the Braddell area its name) was a lawyer who helped prepare the evidence for the court martials. In his 1934 *The Lights of Singapore* book, he noted: 'The whole thing was so senseless and so wicked; these brave fellows were just cat's-paws, persuaded by lies into the doing of something that never could have had the slightest chance of success ... It is all a bad memory, and the sooner it is forgotten, the better.'

Misguided stooges ...

Only the Europeans, it may be noted, were really shaken by the Sepoy Mutiny. The mutineers had made it their business to point their guns at white faces alone, demanding further to know if the Caucasians they encountered were 'Inglees'. Braddell opined that around the area of Alexandra Road and Ayer Rajah Road, 'many ghosts must walk, for these roads formed the scene of the terrible mutiny of 1915, when over 40 white people were done to death.'

Most of those white fatalities were buried at Bididari Cemetery. Twenty-three of them were full or part-time military who were given a formal military service on 3 April with a firing party of 200 letting off three volleys in salute. These 23 are further commemorated by plaques in St Andrew's Cathedral. Another plaque in Victoria Memorial Hall contained the names of all 40 people killed by the mutineers (including the two Chinese and one Malay).

In February and March, a grateful Governor Sir Arthur Young staged three special parades on the Padang in front of the Singapore Cricket Club pavilion to personally thank the sailors of the French, Japanese and Russian navies who had left their ships in the harbour to help quell the mutiny.

A speech given at the Memorial Hall on 28 September 1915 before Sir Arthur by a fevered Mr Frank Adam still insisted the hand of the Kaiser was behind the mutiny. Mr Adam described the Hall's plaque as 'a milestone which will for ever stand in our midst as a reminder of what German frightfulness has done and what it is still capable of doing.'

Mr Adam then explained why only the military victims were being thus commemorated. 'Owing to the fact that the fallen were of Asiatic as well as of European nationality, and also because they belonged to so many races and creeds, it was felt that the placing of a memorial to them in any place of worship would be inappropriate.' Quite ...

Five Kings of
Ancient Singapura

Fort Canning Hill

Who lies buried in the mysterious tomb
on the Forbidden Hill? Is it Singapura's final
king ... or someone else?

It's had many names during its 700-odd known years. It's a
spot drenched in history like no place else in Singapore. It's
Fort Canning Hill.

Now a quiet part of town, it can tell stirring tales of ancient
Singapura's five kings, their royal concubines, visits from
China's dynastic explorers, battles between rival Malays,
Javanese, Sumatrans and Siamese – and durian trees.

These stirring tales (excepting those durian trees) were
chronicled in *Sejarah Melayu* or *Malay Annals*.
Told in 34 episodes, these annals were **Stirring tales ...**
written by 15th century Malaccan court
scholars to give an official account of the Malay-Malaccan
'Golden Era' royal lineage. Meaning that, like Shakespeare's
historical plays, they were written to please royal masters, to
justify and affirm the version of history these royals wished to
pass down through the ages to posterity.

Including, some 400 years later, to Stamford Raffles. His
own copy is now in the National Museum, which knows it as
Raffles Manuscript 18. In these annals, episodes one to six
deal with Singapore – with the third one (over-excitedly?)
describing mid-14th century Singapura thus: 'A great city to
which foreigners resorted in great numbers so that the fame
of the city and its greatness spread throughout the world'.

As Raffles wrote to London, in a letter dated 10 June 1819:
'But for my Malay studies, I should hardly have known that
such a place (i.e. Singapore) existed.'

Nila Utama's 'Lion'

The story begins nearly 700 years ago, with a Sumatran prince setting out northwards from the crumbling royal Srivijaya court at Palembang in search of new territory. His boat dropped anchor at Bintan, from where he spied another island close by. He was informed this was Temasek, inhabited by a handful of *orang laut*. He decided to explore it. The year was very possibly 1299. The prince was Nila Utama. And Temasek was about to get a new name.

For Nila Utama, as the renowned story goes, insisted the fierce wild beast he spotted soon after landing on Temasek

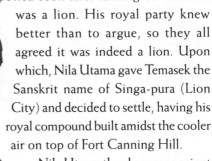

was a lion. His royal party knew better than to argue, so they all agreed it was indeed a lion. Upon which, Nila Utama gave Temasek the Sanskrit name of Singa-pura (Lion City) and decided to settle, having his royal compound built amidst the cooler air on top of Fort Canning Hill.

Nila Utama thus became ancient Singapura's first king, and was happy to receive tribute from friendly passers-by. Such as a traveller from China named Wang Dayuan who called the hill Banzu and who wrote of Temasek's small community: 'They wear their hair short, with turbans of gold-brocaded satin and red oiled clothes covering their bodies.'

Nila Utama was not so happy to receive attention from hostile passers-by, such as a 70-boat Siamese invading party which in about 1325 laid siege to the Fort Canning Hill compound for a month. This was lifted only by the chance arrival at Dan-ma-xi (then a Chinese name for Singapura) of a well-protected imperial envoy from China, where the Mongol Yuan dynasty was encouraging its traders to roam the southern seas.

Nila Utama died in 1347, whereupon his elder son Paduka Sri Pikrama Wira took over and saw his little island kingdom continue to thrive and flourish – and continue to attract envy from other powers in the region.

Envious neighbours ...

Especially from Java, which sent a force to crush the upstart state. Precise details of the conflict are unknown because the *Malay Annals* in its wisdom decided to do some fast-forwarding: 'The history of the war between Singapura and Java is a long one. If we related it all, the people who heard it would be bored; wherefore we abbreviate it, for a slow and long-drawn-out narrative would not be pleasing to people of intelligence.'

Fair enough but the outcome is known: Java was resisted this time round. Sri Pikrama then felt obliged to seek the umbrella protection of that previously hostile Siamese kingdom, as China's new Ming dynasty (installed in 1368) had ordered Chinese withdrawal from Nanyang. He went on to enjoy a reign of 12 years, before being succeeded by his son Sri Rana Wikerma.

King number four was Dam Raja, who reigned from 1375–1388 and who was then succeeded by his son Iskandar Shah. Or so the official version that is the *Malay Annals* would have posterity believe.

Chinese and Portuguese Versions

A different version can be pieced together from Chinese and Portuguese accounts of Iskandar Shah (a Malay adaptation of the name Alexander the Great, the widely-admired Macedonian warrior-king). These suggest that Singapura's fifth king had no kinship link with Sumatra's Srivijaya royalty, but was actually a justice-fleeing rascal from Java who murdered Dam Raja and usurped his place upon Fort Canning Hill!

Cape of Stakes

The popular, if unlikely, version of how Tanjong Pagar – Malay for 'Cape of Stakes' – got its name dates from Dam Raja's reign. Seems that Singapura was then mightily perturbed by 'flying swordfish', one of which even ripped the royal cloak of Dam Raja while he went to the seafront to see this menace for himself. The problem was solved by a bright-spark 11-year-old boy who suggested putting a fence with sharpened tops along the afflicted coastline. Banana tree wood was spiked and put in place. Sure enough, swordfish 'in their thousands' impaled themselves, the problem was over and Tanjong Pagar got its name.

But no happy ending for the boy. The street-smart youngster so worried Dam Raja's jealous inner circle, they advised the ruler: 'If that boy is so clever now, he will become a peril to his betters when he grows up.' The ruler lamely agreed, and ordered him put to death. Which goes to show, does it not, that it doesn't always pay to strive for too much excellence, too soon.

Whatever, his reign was not to be a long one. For in 1392, a Javanese force returned to attack Singapura and made no mistake, second time round. The invaders had insider help from the outraged father of the woman Iskandar had made his chief concubine. For the king had her executed when he chose to believe jealous rumours from his lesser concubines that she'd been unfaithful to him.

The Javanese were not after new conquests. They crudely devastated Singapura and its hilltop royal compound, then moved on – thus plunging the island into the historical obscurity from which it would not be plucked until Raffles arrived in 1819.

For his part, Iskandar escaped via Seletar and Muar to Malacca, where he initiated its sultanate in 1393. To Malaccans, Iskandar is better known as Parameswara, and his undignified retreat from Singapura is regarded there as a historic voyage that launched Malacca's own Golden Age. This was to last just over 110 years, helped by the third Ming emperor changing China's trade policy yet again and sending out the noted eunuch-admiral Cheng Ho (he of seven Indian Ocean voyages between 1405–1431 fame) to set his dainty feet on Malaccan soil and use the thriving spice-trade town as his supply base camp.

Indeed, during the 15th century, Malacca was allegedly home to some 100,000 people who spoke 84 languages and who established the town as the region's number one. But Malacca's fame attracted other, less welcome visitors from Europe. In 1511, a Portuguese invading force conquered the town (in the process, destroying the now-recreated Sultan's Palace). The Dutch took over in 1641, with the British taking their turn in 1824 (as part of a trade-off with the Dutch for British possessions in Indonesia – and for leaving alone the fledging British port of Singapore).

The Mystery of the Tomb on the Hill

So much then did Iskandar Shah's hasty retreat from Singapura in 1392 set in motion. So how then, is Fort Canning Hill's royal tomb to be explained?

This *kramat* is halfway up the hill, directly up from the Registry of Marriages. It is well cared for by admirers who treat it as a royal tomb, decorated with the Malay royal colour of yellow and with lavish flower displays. In 1990, craftsmen gave it a canopy shelter held up by 20 carved wood columns (with fighting cock motifs) in a $147,000 restoration project. All because many consider it the resting place of Iskandar Shah, Singapura's fifth and final king.

When Singapore's first British Resident William Farquhar ordered that the trees and thick undergrowth of Bukit Larangan (Malay for Forbidden Hill, as it was then known) be cleared in 1820, his Malay workforce stopped work when they uncovered the *kramat*. Insisting this was a royal tomb, they said the hill was not meant to be walked upon by commoners.

Farquhar had to summon Malaccan workmen to finish the clearing task, after which he had a cannon hauled up to the hilltop. This was fired a dozen times, then a Union Jack was hoisted up a flagpole – and the hill's 'forbidden' mystique thereby dispelled.

Dispelling the mystique ...

Farquhar's replacement John Crawfurd was sensitive to the hilltop's historical significance after discovering the royal compound's baked-brick foundations and other 'relics of antiquity'. Such relics are still being found in modern times, with pieces of glass, Chinese porcelain, Malay pottery, Javanese jewellery, brass coins and even flecks of gold being unearthed in archaeological digs.

Crawfurd also admired the orchard those ancient kings had cultivated: 'Here we found the durian, the rambutan, the dukun, the pomelo and other fruit trees of great size.'

Stamford Raffles had Bukit Larangan prosaically renamed as Government Hill, and ordered his Government House ('a small bungalow') built on top. He enjoyed the air up there and the view: '... though the height is inconsiderable, we find a great difference in climate. Nothing can be more beautiful than the view from this spot.'

Raffles also showed respect for that royal *kramat*. In a 1823 letter to London, Raffles wrote that should he die in Singapore, he would be content if his body 'had the honour of mixing with the ashes of the Malayan kings'. In fact, Raffles died far from Government Hill – back in his home village of Hendon to the northwest of London, and was buried English-style at his parish church of St Mary's in 1826.

Yet despite Raffles's romanticism, it is unlikely that the *kramat* contains the ashes of any ancient Singapura king – and certainly not Iskandar Shah. The dull truth is that the identity of the *kramat's* 'resident' is utterly unknown.

Taking on a Military Role

A hilltop fort went up in 1861, requiring the demolition of Raffles's bungalow (of which no precise visual record exists). This fort was deemed necessary because of the British Empire's sudden insecurities after the 1857 India Mutiny. The hilltop was levelled and seven 68-pounder guns placed there, facing the sea. The hill was given its current name in honour of India's then governor-general, Viscount George Canning.

The Battle Box

Fort Canning Hill's Command Centre was commonly known as the 'Battle Box'. A sweat-inducing nine metres underground, it was a labyrinth of passageways with 24 separate operation rooms.

As part of the 1992 activities to mark the 50th anniversary of Singapore's fall, the Battle Box was spruced up and opened to visitors. It was in almost exactly the same internal state as that grim Sunday in February 1942 when Lt-Gen Percival emerged after deciding at a 9.30 am meeting that dwindling water and food supplies meant Britain must surrender Singapore to Japan.

The Debate Rages On

Who rests within Canning Hill's kramat may prove a permanent controversy. In 1997, a series of scholars and historians argued the case in *The Straits Times* – with no agreement on whether the first ancient king or the fifth or no-one royal at all lies buried there.

Fort Canning ceased its military function in 1907 and by 1927, the top of the hill had been converted into a reservoir. Then in 1936, as Japan's warlike noises rumbled rapidly into warlike actions, a sprawling underground bunker fortress was dug into the hilltop to serve as Command Centre headquarters for British military operations in Southeast Asia.

Today's Fort Canning Hill, as befits its long and rich history, is many things, including a home for the arts, with bases for the TheatreWorks drama group and Singapore Dance Theatre as well as hosting an Asean Sculpture Garden. Its quiet and coolish hilltop is also one of Singapore's top five 'lover's lane' spots for a spot of private kissing and cuddling. Nila Utama might have been surprised if he could have foreseen 700 years into the future. There again, if he really did think he'd seen a lion somewhere near today's Padang, maybe nothing would have surprised him ...

Drama Under the Stars

The ex-National Theatre
Fort Canning Park, Clemenceau Avenue

Opened in 1963, the theatre on the park would face much criticism till its demise more than 20 years later.

Amazingly, the National Theatre still figures on the occasional tourist map of Singapore. It's shown (alongside the aquarium) on the fringe of Fort Canning Park by Clemenceau Avenue, that bit of the park which was lopped off for the CTE extension.

Actually, this National Theatre was demolished in August 1986. It had a distinctive soaring front section facing River Valley Road, described by architect-writers Edwards and Keys as 'a somewhat ungainly composition of lozenge-shaped, reinforced concrete motifs, filled with brickwork and hardly in keeping with the building's parkland setting.' This peaked with five concrete points which, set against a crescent-shaped

The National Theatre stood proudly for over 20 years, despite its many critics.

fountain in front, were intended to evoke the central symbol of the national flag.

The theatre was commissioned in 1959 as a 'permanent memorial' to Singapore's arrival at self-government. Then Culture Minister S. Rajaratnam said it was meant as a symbol 'affirming the people's faith in their ability to create a Malayan nation and culture.' It was also meant to be the region's 'finest open-air national theatre'.

It cost some $2.2 million to build, with $850,000 of that coming from the public in a unique 'dollar-a-brick' scheme. It was officially opened in August 1963 for a Southeast Asian Cultural Festival, and finally completed in February the next year.

A 'dollar-a-brick' scheme ...

Public idealism aside, the National Theatre (or Panggong Negara, as it was officially called) ran into criticism almost right away, being dubbed in some unkind quarters a 'white elephant' – especially as far as classical music concerts were concerned.

For its open-air aspect made it difficult to keep the sound acoustics under control. And when visitors such as the London Philharmonic Orchestra came to play in their stiff black tails and bow ties, they found the stifling night air far too uncomfortably sweat inducing to give of their musical best.

Other problems emerged. The very idea of an open-air theatre in the local climate was mocked, even if distinguished ballerina Dame Margot Fonteyn did insist in a 1971 interview: 'I love this theatre. I think it is the perfect one for this sort of climate.'

Of Roosting Birds and Hungry Cockroaches

In fact, the noise from the surrounding road traffic was a further distraction. Birds would roost in the beams of the canopy-style steel roof and deposit their droppings on the 3,400 seats below. Packs of cockroaches would wander freely among the rows of chairs. The occasional rat would scurry across the auditorium, disconcerting all bar the most intense theatre-goer.

It was all a bit much. A public debate took off in the early 1980s on the future of this troubled theatre in the park. Some argued its national symbolism should ensure its survival after improvements. Others said it had not been meant anyhow for 'posh' events like classical music concerts and ballet. Mr Alfred Wong, its designer, had some bold comments to offer, too.

He said: 'People have forgotten that this was the first major public building put up after the PAP government came into power. It was built with public subscription, with money from rickshaw pullers to coolies. The intention was that everybody at grassroots level would feel that they were putting up this cultural theatre. No other building in Singapore was put up this way.'

Then Mr Wong insisted, bravely or foolishly: 'With routine maintenance, the building, as with other steel structures like the Eiffel Tower and the Sydney Harbour Bridge, will last for a good many years.'

Ironically for Mr Wong, it was that 150-tonne cantilevered steel roof that proved the National Theatre's undoing. It was ruled structurally unsafe, especially as piling work had just been announced for the CTE extension so close by. Its proposed demise drew forth critical acclaim. A *Sunday Times* editorial opined: 'It's inelegant to the point of being ugly, the acoustics are nothing to shout about, and the stage tends to swallow up troupes any smaller than a Cecil B. de Mille cast of thousands.'

Even if it did drip with the symbolism of Singapore's young nationhood and uneasy two-year existence within the bosom of Malaysia, even if it had been used for National Day rallies, the National Theatre had to go. New money would be diverted into making the Kallang Theatre the main theatre in town.

Lucky Numbers

Helping the cultural cause was the Singapore Sweep with its monthly prize draws and 'Together, Let's Build the Esplanade – Theatres On the Bay' message. Plus, the hope that the Esplanade would visually do for Singapore what its Opera House has so magnificently achieved for Sydney.

The National Theatre put on its last show on 15 January 1984 (having to cancel a booking for *Fiddler On the Roof*). By August 1986, it had been totally demolished and excised from Fort Canning Park – if not from some present-day tourist maps.

The performing arts scene in Singapore now awaits the emergence by year 2001 of The Esplanade, the charmingly-titled world-class multipurpose $450 million waterfront arts centre with its five main halls on a thin five-hectare strip along Marina Bay opposite The Oriental Hotel. Not forgetting its new Satay Club, jutting out into the bay …

Forgotten Founder

Major-General William Farquhar
National Museum, Stamford Road

Highly regarded by the earliest Chinese community,
does Singapore's first Resident deserve more
recognition for jumpstarting modern Singapore?

It counts as one of the National Museum's most precious historical items. It's the magnificent silver candlestick holder (called 'epergne' by posh sorts) that was commissioned by a thankful Chinese community here for presentation to Singapore's first Resident, Major-General William Farquhar, upon his (enforced) return back to Britain in 1823.

The candlestick holder, created by a leading London silversmith, has an 1825 silver hallmark and is engraved with a Latin motto meaning something odd like: 'I stand, I fall, with my faith and my arms'. It was bought by the National Museum for about $50,000 in 1993 by private sale at Sotheby's London, after it had been put up for auction by Captain David Farquhar Atkins, a direct descendant of Singapore's Farquhar.

William Farquhar may well have been Singapore's original *ang mo*. For he was certainly the first red-haired Caucasian to step ashore here that January day in 1819 when he arrived with Stamford Raffles. Farquhar would become the island's first Resident, serving from 1819–1823 and it was his efforts allied to Raffles's vision that got the show up and running so quickly.

Yet around modern Singapore, there's much Raffles this, Raffles that, Stamford such-and-such and so on. But no Farquhar whatevers. Apart, that is, from a tiny (now vanished!) backstreet off Beach Road, running directly behind the 7th Storey Hotel. Why so little to mark the man of whom the earliest Chinese community evidently thought so highly?

Actually, it has long been a debate in academic and not-so-academic circles whether Farquhar deserved more recognition for his early efforts – or whether Raffles was right to 'sack' him as one incapable of enacting his edicts properly. Modern history has already made its ruling: the absence in the phone book of anything much connected with Farquhar's name tells much.

William Farquhar was born in Perth, Scotland in 1770. When 21 years of age, he made his first major journey east, arriving in Madras as a keen young soldier. He fought in many battles around India, building up an impressive military reputation. Then, as a chief engineer, he took part in the 1795 military excursion that wrested Malacca from Dutch control and stayed put.

The East India Company placed him in charge of Malacca: he was to live there for some 23 years, becoming known locally as the town's 'Rajah'. In effect, he went native in Malacca – learning Malay, marrying a Malay woman and enjoying its easy-going ways. Farquhar found himself increasingly unambitious in any gung-ho imperialistic sense. Besides, he liked Malacca.

Enter Stamford Raffles. The two men had first met when Raffles visited Malacca in 1808 with an order from the British High Command in Calcutta: **Destroy Malacca!** destroy Malacca! The reason? Commerce. It seems that Penang merchants did not appreciate this rival British trading post and had persuaded the East India Company to pull down Malacca's public and commercial buildings, then relocate its traders to Penang, or Prince of Wales Island, as it was then known.

Raffles allowed himself to be talked out of this destructive plan by Farquhar. In his turn, Raffles persuaded the East India Company that when the British had supplanted the Dutch in Malacca, they had pledged to protect its people and its interests.

An Englishman's word was his bond, after all (usually). Raffles pleaded to his superiors: 'A city of such historic importance should not be destroyed. And destroying the homes of 20,000 Melaka people and uprooting them from their homeland, where they and their forefathers have lived for centuries, will be a cruel blow to them'.

Thus was over-ambitious Penang thwarted, and thus is today Malaysia Tourism able to boast of its historically-rich Malacca: 'Where it all began'.

The Great Adventure Begins

When Farquhar was about to set off back to his native Scotland in retirement, Raffles persuaded him to join in his great adventure. And at this earliest of stages, the disputes already begin. We are asked to picture a scene where the two men visualised where their new trading colony should be. Farquhar was all on for the Carimon Islands, Raffles fancied Johor.

Neither proved suitable, so they chose Singapore. In later years, Farquhar – bitter at his 'go home' order from Raffles – would be writing to anywhere that would publish his words, claiming that it was his idea, not Raffles's, to try the island of Singapore. His arguments were even reprinted in the colony's first newspaper, *The Singapore Chronicle* (set up in 1831 admittedly by Farquhar's brother-in-law, F.J. Bernard, noted once by the tiny Bernard Street alongside Farquhar Street).

Heavy guns have, however, scored direct hits on Farquhar's 'I chose Singapore' claim, including a broadside from Lady Sophia Raffles herself. She had letters to prove that her husband was already perfectly aware of what and where Singapore was (from reading the *Malay Annals*) and how he had already decided upon it, taking that slight detour south for a look at the Carimon Islands only to oblige Farquhar.

The most bitter dispute between the two men exploded upon the latter's return to the island in October 1822 after a three-year absence. Raffles found that his appointed Resident was not following the well-detailed plans he had laid down for Singapore.

In particular, Farquhar had shifted the European business centre to Kampong Glam rather than where Raffles had wanted it – around today's Raffles Place. Raffles argued that the swampy land then on the west side of the Singapore river would never be developed if the Europeans didn't set about the task, and he had a hillock flattened to firm up this area's (today's business centre) foundations.

Yet it wasn't as if Farquhar had done little except swing in his hammock during the three years while the main man was away. Large sweeps of thick jungle growth had been cleared under Farquhar's directions. His appeals for traders to come to duty-free, well-protected Singapore and give the place a quick kick-start proved successful. Within a year, its population had expanded to 12,000 or so. And Singapore was on its way.

It was the differences between the two men's personalities that rent them asunder. Farquhar: easy-going, benevolent, almost native; Raffles: stern, in a hurry, convinced he was always right and frankly, rather prim.

Crucial differences in personalities ...

For example, in February 1823, with Forbidden Hill renamed Government Hill, Raffles issued an edict that, not for the only time, finds an echo in the administration of today's Singapore. He wanted firecrackers banned. For the Chinese were too prone, he grumbled, to letting firecrackers off near the hill's *kramat*. This ill-behoved the required dignity of a spot 'so close to the site which has been set aside for the residence of the chief authority'.

In other words, himself – for he was living there at the time. The stiffness of his note was echoed by the fact that Raffles had got his secretary to write it; relations between the two men were well strained by this point. 'The Lieutenant-Governor (i.e. Raffles) desires me to state that he was disturbed during the whole of last night by the nuisance complained of.'

Another quarrel: Farquhar was personally not fussed by gambling (mainly, cockfighting), reasoning that the Chinese liked doing so anyhow, so why not – and besides, it raised money for the administration's coffers. Raffles would have none of this. In May 1823, he overruled Farquhar thus: 'Whoever games for money or goods shall receive 80 blows with a cudgel on the breech.'

Ironically, the man who would replace Farquhar as Resident, John Crawfurd (another Scot), had within a month written to seek an overthrow of the harsh Raffles anti-gambling edict, as he also believed it preferable to control and raise revenue from the gambling that would only, as he and Farquhar both realised, continue in some other shape or form.

One last matter on the town-planning divide between the two men. Farquhar had his home on what sounds like the SCC end of today's Padang. Raffles wanted this open space built over and developed, but it was Farquhar who persuaded the early Europeans to build their houses around it and thus preserve the open space we now treasure so much as the Padang.

On a more personal issue, Raffles noted that his Resident was 'particularly subject to native influence and controlled by native ideas.' Raffles was in general deeply sympathetic to the cultures and ways he encountered during his years in Southeast Asia. But he did feel that the white man had a certain (superior) distance to keep. Farquhar for his part not only had a Malay

Bye-bye, Raffles

What turned out to be Raffles's final public function here came in 1823 when he laid the foundation stone for the Singapore Institute (now known as Raffles Institution). Raffles intended it 'for the cultivation of Chinese and Malayan literature, and for the moral and intellectual improvement of the archipelago.' Raffles chose the school's site himself, by 'Bras Bussa creek'. It was forced to relocate in 1972, following demolition to make way for Raffles City.

Tangling with Singapore's Fauna

During the earliest days of Farquhar's residency, there was a major menace: rats. Thousands of them and huge, too. The cats the Europeans had brought with them just could not handle the numbers. Raffles's Malay chronicler Munshi Abdullah even recounted one incident when a cat was pinned down by six or seven rats, and had to be rescued by human intervention. And when the rats starting swarming through Farquhar's own home at night, his patience snapped.

He issued a decree: One *wang* for every rat. At this distance, the value of a *wang* is unclear but it must have been desirable as the townspeople went berserk making rat-traps. Every day, people brought their dead rats to Farquhar's door. Some had 50 or 60, some just a half-dozen. Soon there were thousands, and Farquhar ordered the digging of a deep trench to hold all the dead rats.

But a week later, there were still rats, so Farquhar upped the price for each dead one. This finished the rodents off, for soon there were no more to be found. They had actually been wiped out.

Wait, for then there was a new animal menace. Giant centipedes which kept falling from attap roofs while people were sleeping, much to their discomfort as these creatures could have a nasty bite. Again, the prize was one *wang*, and again Farquhar had a daily delivery of hundreds of dead creatures. And again, they were pretty much exterminated.

Then, a personal animal tragedy for Farquhar. He was fond of taking strolls around the swelling Singapore, often accompanied by his dog. On one such occasion, he was walking alongside the Rochor river when his dog jumped in for a swim. Alas, the pooch was seized by a 5 m-long crocodile. This was the first occasion that the early Europeans even realised the waters of Singapore contained crocodiles.

> Farquhar took immediate action. He ordered the river dammed and the crocodile trapped. It was soon speared to death. No decent burial was allowed. Farquhar ordered that its corpse be strung up upon a semi-sacred banyan tree by the Bras Basah river or, as we know it now, the Stamford canal. Presumably this was meant as a lesson to other crocodiles that handbags and belts were their only future if they strayed out of line.

wife, he also went around dressed in a sarong! As Raffles complained, Farquhar had moved away from 'the usual etiquette in dispensing with the military dress of his rank.'

There was, however, one occasion when Raffles conspicuously did give public support to his Resident. In March 1823, Farquhar had been stabbed in the chest by one Sayid Yasin whom he had imprisoned for failure to pay a debt. Yasin was killed on the spot, bayonetted so savagely his body was scarcely **Killed on the spot ...** recognisable. Raffles then ordered that the corpse be hung up in an iron cage at Telok Ayer for a decomposing fortnight before any burial could take place. This was less a personal backing for Farquhar, more the stern Raffles way of instilling respect for the British administration.

Auld Lang Syne

For taming Fort Canning Hill, for preserving the Padang, for ridding the place of its rats and centipedes and of course, for the personal loss when his dog was crunched between a crocodile's jaws, Farquhar deserves his place in Singapore history.

And more than just a single street name. He was undoubtedly a popular man, as the warmth according his departure in September 1823 records. Farquhar left behind a sense of friendship, Raffles a sense of respect. Which probably sums up best the difference between the two men.

Thousands saw Farquhar off. According to Abdullah: 'The appearance of the scene was as a father among his children. All were weeping; he wept also. "Selamat!" they cried. "Sail with a good wind, that you may arrive at your country to see your parents and relatives! Selamat again! Long life to you that you may come back to be our Governor!" '

Song Ong Siang noted in his book *100 Years' History of the Chinese in Singapore*: 'Farquhar had tried to look at Asiatic problems through Asiatic spectacles and failed as an administrator of the high-principled policy laid down for him by Raffles.'

Through Asiatic spectacles ...

Or, as Raffles preferred to put it in one of his many 1823 letters aimed at justifying his removal of Farquhar: 'However competent that officer may have been for the charge in the earlier stage of the Settlement, it is obvious that it has for some time past grown beyond his management.'

In another (later) letter, Raffles was anxious to put on record that there was nothing personal in his criticisms: 'I had only one object in view, the interests of Singapore, and if a brother had been opposed to them I must have acted as I did towards Colonel Farquhar, for whom I ever had, and still retain, a warm personal affection and regard. I upheld him as long as I could, and many were the sacrifices I made to prevent a rupture.'

Which was not the way Farquhar saw it. Even if he was made a Major-General as a reward for service before setting off for home. Back in Scotland, he probably had too much time on his hands to muse on his memories and nurse his resentment that the Singapore Story would be written with his name just a footnote in its early history.

He died in Perth in May 1839, at the age of 69. His candlestick holder now in the National Museum shows how much those who knew him, appreciated him personally – and his work for the infant Singapore.

The Orchard Road Area

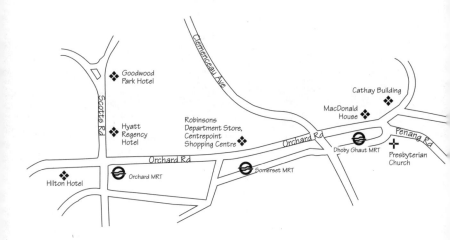

The Door Gods of Orchard Road

Ceramic statues
Hilton International Hotel, 581 Orchard Road

A Tang Dynasty dynamic duo stands guard against
ghosts, evil spirits and whatnots ...

They stand there, fierce and enormous, outside the Hilton with a Häagen-Dazs ice-cream stall in between (such juxtaposition, so Singaporean). These two door gods were once fierce and enormous inside the Hilton but too much so for the hotel's lobby, where they almost touched the ceiling and tended to frighten those of a nervous disposition. Even those who weren't trying to skip out without paying their mini-bar bills.

Now the two brutes are a familiar sight to Orchard Road bouvelardiers, and must crop up as backdrops in many tourist photographs, adding a touch of oriental exoticism. But these guys are no mere ornamentation; they are there – and in a very bad mood – for a reason.

Topnotch ghostbuster – General Qin.

87

Murder in a Hilton Suite

The Hilton's two door gods arrived just too late to have an influence on one of Singapore's most extraordinary murder cases, a murder that went unreported for nearly two years. The victim was Thai-born 44-year-old Mrs Linda Culley, nee Amphumanthana. The murderer was her British husband, Michael Charles Culley, 48.

The murder took place in May 1974 in the Hilton's Suite 1403/04. The body was dumped in a blue wooden trunk which was moved out on the late afternoon of the murder from the hotel, and into a waiting removal van, then transferred to a flat Mr Culley had rented in Cairnhill Court. The corpse in its heavy but loosely-packed trunk had been carried through the hotel lobby and out onto busy Orchard Road without anyone – not even the removal men – noticing anything odd.

Mr Culley continued to stay at the Hilton (having moved into room 615) for a further six or so weeks before relocating to the Cairnhill Court flat. There, he had already dismembered the remains of his dead wife's body, using a hacksaw and an axe, into 13 separate pieces.

These he had put into four large cardboard boxes which were carefully wrapped ('expertly', police were to say, with smell-proof sheets of fibreglass, plywood and trifoam boards) and then 'stored' in a cement-sealed, heavy-duty silver-painted trunk which was left on the flat's outside back balcony. This trunk would take police over an hour to prise open with crowbars, chisels and hammers before the awful stench of two-year-old decomposed human body parts hit their unprotected noses.

The police were called in only after a remarkable confession by the Culleys' then 16-year-old son Charles Leonard on 21 April 1976. His father had just died in a Melbourne hospital of a heart attack but not before telling his Singapore-based son to 'throw the trunk with the body into the sea' and leave immediately for England without saying a word.

Charles, a student at United World College, had lived in the flat with the dismembered corpse of his mother for nearly two years. But upon his father's death, he finally approached the Singapore police accompanied by David Marshall (then the top criminal lawyer here, and later to become Singapore's ambassador to France) as his legal advisor.

Charles admitted that on the evening of the murder in the Hilton's hotel suite (he was then a 14-year-old), his father made this dramatic announcement to him when he came back from school: 'I've killed your mother.' Mr Culley insisted that Charles tell people he had divorced his wife and she had gone back to Thailand. He added that he'd strangled his wife – 'I couldn't help it' – and it took him about 45 minutes to an hour ('a terrible experience') to kill her. Charles noticed that there were no signs of a violent struggle nor blood stains in the hotel suite.

He had committed a serious technical offence by failing to disclose that a murder had taken place but the legal process took a lenient view towards the orphaned teenager, who would return to England to try and start a new life after his gory experiences in Singapore. A verdict of murder was recorded against Michael Culley in January 1977. By which time, of course, he was far beyond the reach of the law.

The book was thus closed on this shocking murder which had taken place in the Hilton – and which went unreported for nearly two years …

The duo represent real-life characters from China's Tang dynasty (A.D. 618–907). One is Wei Chi Jing De, a warlike general who was right-hand man to Emperor Tang Tai Zong. The two weapons in his fists look like batons or rotans but are probably 'peans', an ancient Chinese form of whip – the painful application being a noted skill of Wei's.

His companion is Qin Sho Bao, who was the same emperor's trusty swordsman, as indicated by the two swords he waves in a general Orchard Road direction. In popular Chinese belief, this dynamic duo have become known as the guardians of doorways, springing from the alleged soothing protection they provided for Emperor Tang at night after he spent many sleepless hours in his bed as evil spirits crowded out his dreams, turning them into nightmares.

In modern terms, the emperor was suffering the pangs of a bad conscience. As he deserved to. His path to top slot in the Tang dynasty was littered, Macbeth-style,

A bad conscience ...

with the bloodied corpses of many people Tai Zong either killed himself or had killed to pursue his relentless ambition.

His nocturnal desperation prompted the emperor to ask his two generals for a solution. They suggested they themselves should guard the palace gates at night. They did. Soon, the emperor was sleeping well again – for such is the power of autosuggestion! A happy man again, he ordered that the generals' facial images, with their most fearsome of expressions, be painted and hung up at the gates of the palace to mount permanent 'guard' against ghosts, evil spirits and whatnots.

This top-level endorsement enshrined Qin Qiong and Wei Chogong in the Chinese popular psyche as the most effective and influential of 'door gods'. They replaced various other popular twosomes whose role as ghostbusters had origins going back well over 2,000 years into the beliefs of ancient China.

'Aw-some' Beginnings for the Gods

The Hilton's duo stand 2.7 metres high, weighing three tonnes each. They were commissioned by the hotel in 1975 from a local Teochew family of Chinese potters with the family name of Aw, who approached their task with awe. They needed to build dedicated kilns with large enough doors to 'cook' the beasts. Eight people worked half a year to mould them and when the task was finished, the Aws insisted there were none larger in the world. They'd cost $10,000 then but it's difficult to fix a price on them now, as most potters would probably refuse to undertake such a mammoth task (unless it was made conspicuously worth their while).

The twosome were moved to outside the hotel in 1981 and have stood guard in their current positions ever since. It may further be noticed that each has between their legs, right at the crucial male juncture, a snarling lion's face. Alas, the significance of this is blurred ...

Geomancy Lives On

Hyatt Regency Hotel
Scotts Road ... and elsewhere

Thriving in Singapore is the art of 'perfect
placing' or what babyboomers/aged hippies
might call 'good vibrations' ...

Singapore: Sophisticated city that has the world's most
pagers/handphones per capita, all-digital phone system,
flat high-definition TV screens, laser discs, ATM machines,
laptop computers, advanced test-tube baby techniques,
microwave ovens, fuzzy logic fridges, intelligent lifts, executive
stress 'burn-out', slick MRT trains, SuperBuses, transferable
country/golf club memberships, auto/CPU-opened garage
gates, CTE road tunnels, 'Megatop' 747-400 aircraft, computer
networks, jarring jargon jingles like 'upgrade', 'cutting edge',
'critical mass', 'worst case scenario', 'segment', 'quality time' ...

Singapore: Superstitious city that calls in
geomancers to help design new offices and **A supersti-**
fix their opening times, that makes more **tious city ...**
babies when the year is 'auspicious' (e.g.,
Dragon very good, Snake/Rabbit not so good), that has fish
tanks in living rooms to soak up 'evil spirits', that loves numbers
with the figure '8', that sees its sophisticated modern women
consult fortune tellers about romance prospects, that sees
mothers consult astrologers to set a superior date for a
daughter's wedding, that advises its bachelor men to abstain
from boring holes in coconuts, lest they find themselves
marrying a widow (or, even worse, a divorcee!) ...

Which is the real Singapore? Answer: Both, at the one and
the same time. Nowhere is this more clear than in the use of
geomancy, or *feng shui* – *'feng'* meaning 'wind' and *'shui'* meaning
'water'. That is, the art of 'perfect placing' or what babyboomers/
aged hippies might call 'good vibrations'.

The ancient Chinese practice of geomancy is based on the core belief that good breath (*'sheng qi'*) can breathe life into a building, and thus enable the business conducted within to thrive. *'Qi'* literally means the breath of the dragon, which tops the animal hierarchy in Chinese mythology. And if the elements around a building are not in harmony, evil influences can result which require geomancy principles to correct. Otherwise, business may go bad, as wealth drains out of the building.

Feng Shui Lessons at the Hyatt

Take the Hyatt Regency Hotel, for example. This swanky hotel opened in 1971 and is constantly being modernised. Its front entrance doors were originally parallel to Scotts Road. Wah, got problem! According to geomancy principles, the fact that these doors were also parallel to the hotel's cashier desk meant that wealth could 'flow out' of the hotel. So, at significant added cost, these front doors were 'put right' – at a distinct angle (some say 32 degrees) to Scotts Road.

Alterations were made also to the posh Pinetree Town and Country Club (built in 1984) on Stevens Road. A screen was built behind the front desk in the entrance lobby to counteract a view of some 'undesirable' external elements and to harmonise the 'qi' of the foyer's twin staircases.

Advertising agency Leo Burnett has employed geomancy principles in its office fittings, so has Electro Magnetic, Republic National Bank of New York (Singapore), Hong Leong Building on Collyer Quay, Yunnan Inn Seafood Restaurant on Clementi Road, First National Bank of Chicago and probably (if discreetly) many other commercial enterprises. Opening times can depend on a geomancer's advice, as well. When the American Club was ready to declare open its new $15 million clubhouse on Claymore Hill on 27 May 1989, it took great

The Numbers Game

And then, there's that figure '8'. In the Cantonese dialect, the sound of the word for 'eight' – '*fatt*' – is similar to the sound of the term for 'good luck'. And '88' (check out the lucky building above) thus infers 'double good luck', and onwards. No matter that in Singapore, Cantonese ranks fourth among the Chinese dialects (unlike Hong Kong where it holds sway), many Chinese people here still invest the figure '8' with all sorts of good feelings and strive to get it into their phone numbers, their car registration numbers, their prices, wherever at all possible.

When the 'magical' date of 8-8-88 arrived on 8 August 1988, the excitement was immense. Singapore's stylish OUB Centre in Raffles Place was finished in 1986 but delayed its official opening until that 8-8-88 date. And the rush of pledged couples to the Registry of Marriages on that date was noticeable. The birth rate surged too, nine months after 8-8-88.

In 1996, a new record was set when a wealthy car-owner paid $118,000 for the registration number of his dreams. Such lucky numbers involve 8, of course, plus 2 (sounds like Cantonese for 'easy') and 9 (sounds like 'longevity'). They steer well clear of the figures 1004 which sound (in Hokkien) like 'every day will die' and 114 which sounds like 'death from starvation'. A Lexus saleswoman said cars with such numbers 'would be hard to sell later'.

Singapore Telecom is still running its sought-after Golden Number service, selling off special numbers for mobiles and pagers, as well as normal phones (bids for such numbers can even reach $20,000).

care to ensure the ceremony took place at exactly 3.22 pm. As the club's president, Mr Clyde Stephens, put it: 'It worked for the Hyatt, so it might work for us. But you wouldn't see this happening if the club was in Houston.'

Geomancy principles are employed inside the home, too. For instance, the cooker ought not to be opposite the washing machine or the sink in the kitchen, for this puts fire and water (two incompatible elements) in direct contrast. Nor should the kitchen door be larger than the main front door, as this disrupts the harmony of the home and may cause an outflow of 'good luck'.

In the bedroom, the sleeping angle/bed position matters, for each room has a 'death point' and a 'wealth point', based on the influence of the magnetic field. There again, a fish

Sleeping angles and bed positions ...

tank or a growing plant (which requires constant watering) can be of a counteracting beneficial effect in the boudoir.

Tombstones also can gain from the good use of geomancy principles, guaranteeing a peaceful afterlife for their occupants by ensuring the forces of water and wind are in harmony. Thus a hilly site is preferred, and the Adam Road cemetery is a striking example of this principle.

Feng Shui Goes West

Geomancy principles found it easy to penetrate the Western world's soft-brained New Age mood leading up to the new millennium. In the UK, a successful new monthly magazine called *The Art of Feng Shui* promised 'all you need to know about enhancing your life at home and work!'. There was some resistance, however, with UK women's mag *Red* asking: '*Feng Shui* - The Biggest Con of the Decade?'

Even so, in 1998, Cherie Blair, big-time lawyer wife of Britain's Prime Minister Mr Tony Blair, gave 10 Downing Street some touches of *feng shui* (such as a fish tank with three goldfish, 'counteracting' the allegedly inauspiciously south-facing if world-famous black front door – and getting Mr Blair to sleep above the shop 'pointing in a northeast direction'). But one London theoretical physics academic, Professor John Charap, snapped back: 'It's a load of codswallop. Cherie Blair is a bit flakey about these things.'

A Costly Consultation

Yet, not everyone is always thrilled with the advice of the geomancer. There was an accountants' meeting in 1988 at which the principles of *feng shui* were discussed, but one of their number (a J. Medora) begged to differ. This dissident recalled an occasion when a Hong Kong geomancy master was summoned to the firm where he once worked.

'At the ceremony, I expected him to go into a trance, or do a dance. Instead he whipped out his calculator, asked for all our birthdays, and it went click, click, click. We were told where we should be seated. But nothing fortuitous happened. And to think that it cost us $1,500 for a few minutes work!'

This hard-headed accountants' meeting also raised the case of the geomancer who insisted his payments always be in units of $36, $72, or $108. He explained these impressive-sounding specifications by saying that when three and six, seven and two, or one and eight were added up, they all came to nine. Which in Chinese sounded like 'long-lasting'.

One example of what was regarded as bad geomancy is the 1934 Hill Street old police station building once used by the government's National Archives and Oral History Department. This handsome building (now

Bad geomancy ...

being restored by PWD) was felt to have spoilt the 'shape' of the area which up to then had apparently resembled that of the *'peh toh'*, or Lunar New Year fish, which is eaten raw and which is held to effect 'good fortune'.

Raw fish is thus favoured because its Cantonese term sounds like 'double happiness'. In Western culture, a rough equivalent would be eating a dish of corned beef hash coated with honey on each January 1. This may sound utterly disgusting but there again, the key words do rhyme with 'cash' and 'money'!

Maybe Shakespeare's wise words from his King Lear would be more useful. 'This is the excellent foppery of the world that, when we are sick in fortune – often the surfeit of our own behaviour – we make guilty of our disasters the sun, the moon and the stars.' This quotation was used by a (Chinese) writer to *The Straits Times* letters page in February 1990.

His conclusion was a plea: 'The *feng shui* paranoia which is afflicting our population must be arrested before it gets out of hand.'

Grand Old Hotel Tales

Goodwood Park Hotel's Eastern Fantasy and
Raffles Hotel's Shanghai Lily

Scotts Road

*Who was the full-bosomed beauty who inspired
the seductive Eastern Fantasy in the
Goodwood Park Hotel?*

An alluring painted temptress tempts within the tower block boardroom of the Goodwood Park Hotel; her full-bosomed pose must have enlivened many private business discussions. Even if only to ask how this seductive Eastern Fantasy came to be in the Goodwood at all, and if it was a real woman who'd inspired this luscious 115 cm x 140 cm painting.

For the answers, those of us not often in the Goodwood's boardroom must go back in time. In 1900, the Teutonia Club had just declared open its Rhineland castle-style tower block (the only rooftop in Singapore designed to cope with snow?) to tastefully dominate Scotts Road. The Teutonia was a social, sporting and cultural club for the 100-plus German community here and fulfilled that role until 1914. Then the outbreak of World War I in Europe saw Singapore's British colonial masters seize everyone and everything German in town as 'enemy property'. Including the Teutonia Club.

When the war was over, the building was sold at auction to three Jewish brothers, the Manassehs (Anglophiles from Calcutta), who turned it into a 'restaurant-cafe-entertainment place' named Goodwood Hall (that Park Hotel bit came later to reflect its new mildly-aristocratic English style with Scottish touches, such as its Gordon Grill).

In 1942, the Goodwood became a residence for senior officers of Japan's Imperial Army. Ezekiel Manasseh was sent to Changi jail where he would die in the prison's hospital. After the war, Ezekiel's Australian stepson Vivian Bath bought out the other two Manasseh brothers' shares and became sole

Goodwood Park Hotel: 'The tales I could tell!'

proprietor of the Goodwood, setting it up as a glitzy and successful rival to Raffles Hotel.

A Russian in The Straits Times

But, but ... How about that Eastern Fantasy? Yes, yes ... She makes her entry at this stage in the story. In 1948, Vivian Bath paid $450 to buy the painting from its creator, Russian artist Vladimir Tretchikoff. He had come to Singapore in 1939 to work as a cartoonist with *The Straits Times* and was post-war to join his family in South Africa where he would prosper hugely as an artist.

Vivian Bath sold off the Goodwood in 1963 and retired to Australia but he left that Eastern Fantasy behind, hanging in the hotel's boardroom. It has never been valued because the hotel has no intention of selling it. As a Goodwood spokes-

'Snowflakes' and Anna Pavlova

Anna Pavlova, the world's most famous ballerina of her time, gave a dance performance at the Goodwood in December 1922. Reluctantly. She was supposed to do her show at the Victoria Hall but a local amateur dramatic society insisted it had a prior booking there to put on a dreary Gilbert & Sullivan evening, and won't give way – no matter how famous Ms Pavlova was.

The ballerina slipped into a bad mood before her first dance *Dying Swan* was through because of how cramped the Goodwood stage was for herself and her 35-strong back-up company. Then during her version of *Coppelia and Snowflakes*, she noticed a well-meaning Chinese stagehand up high above her, shredding pages of white paper and dropping them down to evoke an image of falling snowflakes. Ms Pavlova stopped her dance, and threatened to storm off the stage if bits of paper didn't stop falling on her head.

Ms Pavlova recovered her serenity, carried on and later described her visit here as 'unforgettable', leaving behind $300 for 'a deserving cause in Singapore'. When she next came here, in 1929, the Victoria Hall was wisely put at her disposal.

Anna Pavlova has another lasting memorial – Australia's ghastly meringue-style dessert, know for short as a 'Pav'. It's popular in New Zealand, too, where a 'new cuisine' version uses kiwi and passion fruits as toppings, embedded within 'lashings of whipped cream'. This monstrous Pavlova recipe is available via the publisher!

woman put it: 'The painting is an important part of the hotel's history.'

Then in 1989, remarkably, a Mrs Leonora Schmidt – of mixed Dutch-Indonesian parentage and then a 74-year-old – turned up at the Goodwood

The Eastern Fantasy unveiled!

and revealed that 46 years before, she had been the artist's model for Eastern Fantasy! She had other stories to tell, too. It seems that Tretchikoff had also been working for the British war propaganda effort and wisely decided to flee Singapore in early 1942 on a Java-bound boat just before the Japanese marched in. But he was later that year arrested in Jakarta by the Kempeitai (Japan's secret police) and accused of being the leader of a spy ring. For unclear reasons, Tretchikoff escaped death, was released and was able to stay at liberty in Indonesia for the duration of the war.

It was in Jakarta in 1943 that he painted Eastern Fantasy in 10 days. And what enticed Mrs Schmidt as a 29-year-old to reveal so much of herself for the artist's eye during those troubled years? In 1989, she explained: 'I did it for Tretchi (note: he called her Lenka!). I wouldn't have done it for anyone else. He was a talented artist and I knew it would turn out to be a beautiful painting.'

It did, and it is still a striking piece of work today. It symbolises her European-Asian heritage by contrasting a tailored jacket with a loose sarong, and the traditional Indonesian kris (curved knife) with a Bible. And it was a nice touch that during her 1989 visit Mrs Schmidt gamely posed alongside the portrait of herself as a ripe young woman – it made an excellent newspaper photograph.

She disclosed a further (coincidental) personal link with the Goodwood. As a linguist, she had acted as an interpreter during the war crime tribunals that were held at the Goodwood in 1946. She was also a fortunate woman not to have endured sex slavery during those war years. It only emerged in 1992

The Day Liz Taylor Revealed All at Raffles

There's a long history of rivalry between Goodwood and Raffles (when they were the only two big hotel players in town) over who could boast the most celebrity guests. The Raffles probably edged in front because it had the incidents to go with the big names. Such as the case of Elizabeth Taylor and her evening dress.

Liz was at the Raffles in 1960 accompanying her then husband Mike Todd, whose *Around the World in 80 Days* movie was being launched at Cathay cinema. The hotel put up a dinner in her honour, so Liz naturally wanted a swish party frock for the occasion. She hired one from dressmaker Doris Geddes, who had her 'The Little Shop' in the Raffles Arcade. But during the dinner, the dress (according to an eyewitness) 'fell to bits', causing Ms Taylor much unstylish embarrassment. Later Liz blasted Ms Geddis for her 'shoddy workmanship'. Doris was having none of this. She retorted that Liz was 'too fat'!

It was also at the Raffles that Dr Milton Obote, as the then prime minister of Uganda, was having lunch when he was discreetly informed that he was no longer the prime minister of Uganda. It was January 1971, and Idi Amin had just arrived on the world stage by taking over the top job while Obote was conveniently away in Singapore. And few will forget the scenes in and outside the Raffles in August 1993 when Michael Jackson checked in for his National Stadium concerts. The Weird One hit Singapore just as those child abuse allegations were making world headlines, which meant a world media circus outside the hotel on Beach Road hoping for a Jackson comment and/or photo.

Neither came as the singer stayed firmly tucked away in his suite, allegedly asking that a swimming pool be filled with Evian mineral water for his frolicking and succeeding in persuading Singapore Zoo to send around five of its playful orang-utans for his private entertainment. How did Michael Jackson get in and out of the hotel, away from prying eyes? The explanation emerged later: there's a 'secret' tunnel leading in from the back of the Raffles and connecting with its strictly-private (and very expensive) suites.

that at least 100 Dutch women were forced to work as prostitutes to service Japanese officers during their occupation of Indonesia.

In 1992, one such Dutch woman named Ms Keetje Ruizeveld – then an 86-year-old – broke the silence over this issue in a Dutch newspaper when she said: 'For the young Dutch girls of 16 or 17, it was very difficult. Some wanted to commit suicide.' She conceded that she didn't suffer as much as did Indonesian sex slaves as Caucasian women were, she said, reserved for the officer classes rather than the foot-troops who treated native women with contempt. 'With us, the Japanese were polite people. There were rules in the brothel. For example, they had to shower beforehand.'

Ms Ruizeveld said she'd chosen 'the lesser of two evils' by going into a Japanese-run brothel. 'Some of the women who refused were never seen again. I think they were probably shot.'

The lesser of two evils ...

Mrs Schmidt's personal memories of occupied Java were less troubled. For one thing, her young and voluptuous Eurasian beauty was frozen-in-time for the painting that now hangs in the Goodwood Park Hotel's boardroom, underneath that distinctive Rhineland tower (which was nearly demolished in 1970 and replaced by a 16-storey, 480-room modern hotel block).

A Delightfully Undemure Maiden

If there is another painting in Singapore to rival the sensuous allure offered by Eastern Fantasy, it's the one in the Goodwood's traditional rival, Raffles Hotel, in the curvaceous shape of Tiger Lily, who holds sway behind the bar on the lower level of the hotel's Long Bar.

Lily is not a native of this island. She arrived here only in late-1991 but she has settled in so well that she has a loyal band of male admirers and even a fussy

Long Bar cocktail named in her honour. This bodacious Caucasian woman first appeared on canvas in 1920s' Shanghai (then a racy kind of town) but alas, artist and model remain unknown. The hotel bought the painting locally when looking for ways to pep up its new-style old Long Bar (which reopened in 1991).

Some Tiger Lily observers become amateur art critics as they analyse her shape and proportions. One overheard bar-stool comment grumbled that her head was 'too large' for her body, to which the reply from the bar-stool alongside was that it wasn't the delightfully undemure Tiger Lily's head that had caught his eye.

The Worst Fire Disaster

Robinsons Department Store
Centrepoint Shopping Centre, Orchard Road

In 1972, a disastrous fire at Robinsons Raffles Place
Department Store killed nine people and destroyed
a famous landmark in local shopping.

There's a good reason why the two public entrances to
Raffles Place MRT station are modelled on the old John
Little store facade. And not that of the Robinsons store which
had dominated here when it was the premier shopping zone
and was called Commercial Place. For unhappy memories are
associated with that old Robinsons. It was destroyed (nine
people killed, property worth $21 million ruined) in a disastrous
fire on 21 November 1972.

Soon after the store had opened that morning, a short
circuit caused by a tangle of old electricity wires in the loft
burned through their wire rubber casing, sparking off a blaze.
The burning smell was detected quickly enough and at 10.05,
the first emergency call was received at Central Fire Station
on Hill Street.

Mistakenly judging the problem to be a small and localised
outbreak, just the one fire engine was sent round to the store.
There it discovered that the water pressure from the hydrant
outside Robinsons was too weak for the water hoses, and that
the nearest other hydrant (at Malacca Street) was not
functioning properly.

Suddenly, Robinsons became a major problem. A fire
disaster, no less. Other fire engines rushed to the scene but
met with the same obstacle: weak water pressure. Shoppers
were still fleeing the store when inside, an electricity cut-off
plunged the place into darkness – and forced two lifts to halt
in between floors. Inside these lifts, eight employees (including
a young pregnant woman) would die horribly. A ninth fatality
was found later inside a second-floor toilet.

The public entrance to the Raffles Place MRT station is modelled on the old John Little store facade.

The store seemed to be ill-fated that day. The man in charge of the store's own emergency fire-fighting and lift-rescue team was off-duty. An unauthorised stock of inflammable material had been stored within the loft where the initial short circuit occurred, turning the fire from a controllable outbreak to an unstoppable inferno.

And the store did not have its own anti-fire sprinkler system, despite repeated warnings to this effect from the Fire Service, whose fire engines were held up by a typical morning traffic jam on 21 November 1972. Access was further hindered by double-parked cars in Raffles Place, and more time was wasted by the fireman having to fetch their water from the Singapore river.

The fire ended by burning itself out, leaving just the empty facade of what had been Robinsons. Its now-charred metal logo Mercury statue on top was twisted by the heat into a grotesque mangle. News photos show just how devastating the blaze was and how completely the Robinsons building was gutted.

The Fire Service had to endure much **Coffeeshop** coffeeshop criticism from the public **criticism ...** afterwards, especially because of how it was unable to rescue those suffocating victims from the jammed lifts. One fire-fighter had got near enough to a lift to hear desperate pleas from inside it but the heat was too intense and the smoke too thick for the fire-fighters to get any closer.

It took a special Commission of Enquiry to clear the Fire Service. The Commission ruled that the men had 'fought the fire under trying conditions and had done well in containing the fire from spreading to other buildings in the area'. Also that the fire-fighters had 'discharged their duties commendably'. Essential lessons for both the Fire Service and for in-store safety precautions had been learned in the grimmest way possible.

A Golden Age Remembered

It was the end for Robinsons's 80 years of lording it over Commercial Place as Singapore's premier department store. Even if (in response to a management call to get back into action by that Christmas) it did open up again on 15 December. Only now, it was in Specialists' Centre on Orchard Road, a move its staff felt represented the 'end of an era'.

For Robinsons had been founded in 1858, eight years after John Little (which tagged itself the 'Universal Providers of Singapore') had become the colony's first department store. By 1881, Robinsons had overhauled its rival and opened up new premises on Battery Road. In 1886, its founder Peter Robinson died and his son (given the excessive name of

Stamford Raffles Robinson!) took over, moving the store across the road to Commercial Place in 1891.

In 1935, Stamford Raffles (the storekeeper, not the founder) died and in November 1941, a swish new store opened – only to be hit by Japanese bombs within a month. In 1955, Robinsons got its air-conditioning and finally gobbled up John Little. In 1957, it had another face-lift that would earn it the tag 'handsomest shop in the Far East'. Just 15 years later, it was no more ...

Handsomest shop in the Far East ...

The old Robinsons had always been an exceedingly European store, in which pretty much the only locals were those working behind the counters (Chinese staff were encouraged to wear pigtails and loose trousers so as to appear picturesque and ethnic for European eyes), or servant classes fetching whatnot for their Tuan Besar employers or well-to-do Eurasian/Nonya owners.

As a display manager recalled: 'It was an exclusive store. People dressed up well just to shop there. Nonyas put on their jewellery to show they were somebody.' For European memsahibs, the social calendar of a typical Singapore day might read: shopping at Cold Storage, coffee at Robinsons, and cocktails at Raffles Hotel.

Snooty, old-fashioned Robinsons inevitably found it difficult to thrive in independent Singapore. It appointed its first-ever local general manager only in 1981 and pulled out of a disastrous three-year financial decline (it was forced to lay off 110 workers in 1984) only in 1985. This was two years after the move across Orchard Road to its current position as anchor tenant in Centrepoint, with John Little (by now, very much Robinsons's junior partner) taking over in Specialists' Centre.

From Disaster to Store of the Year
Robinsons's turnaround came when it realised it should pitch itself at local shoppers (with refund policies, etc.), rather than

at the tourists every other store on Orchard Road seemed to be wooing. In 1990, official recognition came that it had finally ditched the millstones of its past when the Singapore Tourism Promotion Board declared Robinsons as Singapore's Store of the Year.

Its deliberately-infrequent 'The Sale Worth Waiting For' impresses shoppers as being an unusually genuine sale for Orchard Road, its link-up with the UK's St Michael's is a thriving success, and John Little has plans to set up in outlying suburban centres. All seems well.

But Robinsons continues to face intense competition from local stores such as Metro and C.K. Tang and such Japanese giants as Isetan and Sogo (Raffles City's Sogo took in $1.5 million during its first day in October 1986 and police were required to control the frenzied shoppers).

Not to mention the enormous Takashimaya at Ngee Ann City. When this opened in August 1993, it took in $5 million in sales during its first four days. Takashimaya is so very huge, it could absorb the voluminous shopping crowd.

One doesn't have to be a highly-paid retailing consultant to suggest that Singapore has become 'over-shopped' – and that a shake-out must be imminent. But Robinsons now occupies a solid niche and, helped by its strong staff loyalty, can argue that a store able to bounce back from a total disaster like that of November 1972 has shown a resilience that should cope with most challenges.

As Seen on TV

The Robinsons fire featured in the plot of retro drama series *Growing Up* as it moved into the early '70s during its fourth TCS season. Vicky Tay, the character played by actress Irin Gan, found herself trapped in the store when the fire broke out.

Certainly, there have been greater civil disasters with higher casualty lists since that Robinsons fire. The Iron Park Gate disaster of 1974, killing 13; the Spryros tanker explosion and fire at Jurong Shipyard, killing 76 workers and injuring 57 others in October 1978; the collapse of the Hotel New World on Serangoon Road in March 1986, killing 33 people.

Yet despite these bigger fatality figures, people who were around when Robinsons burned down remember it clearly. Even if it did represent an older, stiffer Singapore, Robinsons was nonetheless a familiar landmark building that was suddenly no longer there. For many, that felt unsettling.

A Neighbour Declares War

MacDonald House
Orchard Road

In 1965, the fatal climax of the Indonesian
'Konfrontasi' left three people dead and
more than 35 injured.

A mid-afternoon tropical storm raged outside MacDonald House on Orchard Road. Suddenly, there was a dull thud. It sounded like a violent thunderclap. It was actually a bomb. Three people lay dead or dying. At least 35 people were injured, and the building's mezzanine floor was in one almighty mess.

The date was 10 March 1965, and Singapore had just been hit by the 29th terrorist bomb since Indonesia began its bomb attacks on the island on 24 September 1963. This was eight days after Singapore's merger with Malaya, Sarawak and Sabah to form the new Federation of Malaysia – in response to which, some 20,000 angry Indonesians had 'greeted' the opening of Jakarta's Malaysian Embassy.

The 'Konfrontasi' (confrontation), as Jakarta tagged this near-state of war, had been formally declared on 20 January 1963 by the then Indonesian Foreign Minister Dr Subandrio, on behalf of President Achmed Sukarno. It was formally abandoned in 12 August 1966, even if it did effectively end in October 1965 with Sukarno's failing health sparking off the Indonesian army's first coup – and the beginning of a savage end for the numerically-huge Communist Party of Indonesia (PKI), then the third largest in the world.

During the Konfrontasi, 37 bombs hit Singapore over a period of two years. A total of 60 people were killed or injured. The worst single incident was that MacDonald House bomb.

The Straits Times front page of 11 March 1965 screamed: 'Terror bomb kills 2 girls at bank'; its report pieced together the details of the outrage. The bomb had been placed close to the lift and close to the office then occupied by the Australian

High Commission. This led to an early but inaccurate official statement from Canberra that the bomb had been directed at Australia's representatives.

The two immediate fatalities were Mrs Suzie Choo, 36, private secretary to the Hongkong and Shanghai Bank's MacDonald House branch manager, and Miss Juliet Goh, 23, a bank filing clerk. Both women had the lousy luck to be in the office just the other side of the wall from where the bomb exploded at 3.07 pm.

Gruesome Death by Typewriter

They were buried under the wall's rubble. Miss Goh was dug out by Fire Brigade officers who found that her typewriter lever arm had pierced her chest. When they removed it, her blood spurted out and over their uniforms. Her work tool had become the instrument of her death. A third victim, a man trapped by the lift door, died after an unsuccessful emergency operation at SGH.

The damage spread a distance a hundred or so metres on each side of the bank. News photos of the time showed cars parked on or passing by that stretch of Orchard Road with their windows smashed and every neighbouring shop with its windows broken. It was a powerful bomb, a nitroglycerine 25-pounder with a timer fuse.

An official government statement was issued within hours, pointing an accusing finger: 'So long as there are people in our midst ready to utter slogans which encourage our external enemies to believe that there are people sympathetic to the Indonesian cause, so long will our enemies persist and intensify their barbaric acts of violence.'

Prime Minister Lee Kuan Yew was on an official visit to New Zealand at the time. He sent back a public message from Wellington, in which he too put the blame on Indonesian infiltrators. He said: 'Either it was an Indonesian agent who slipped through or a pro-Indonesian extremist type in their employ. If we are to survive, we have to live with this sort of thing.'

Two Indonesian marines were later arrested, charged and convicted of murder arising from the Macdonald House bombing. They were executed by hanging on 17 October 1968, despite pleas for

Execution by hanging ...

clemency from Indonesia. Their bodies were taken back to Jakarta, where they were hailed by a 10,000-strong crowd which waited at the airport and which lined the streets all the way to the Defence and Security Headquarters building, where the two executed marines lay in state.

Indonesia officially recognised that the marines had operated under the orders of the by-then deposed and semi-disgraced President Sukarno, but public feelings still ran high – and inevitably, boiled over. Some 400 students ransacked Jakarta's Singapore Embassy in retaliation, before moving on to wreck the consul's residence and the homes of two other Singaporean diplomats, while publicly burning the Singapore flag to the delight of a cheering crowd.

The then Foreign Affairs Minister, Mr S. Rajaratnam, said while he sympathised with Indonesia's feelings about the two marines (because they had effectively operated under a previous, now discredited Indonesian regime), Singapore had no alternative but to see the executions through: 'We did what we had to do.'

Explosions in Katong

The first three bombs of the Konfrontasi had gone off in Katong, with the first exploding opposite the old Ambassador Hotel (then Duke, then Katong Park Hotel) in Meyer Road on 24 September 1963. The bombs continued at regular intervals. On 8 March 1964, one went off in a drainpipe attached to Raffles Hotel, badly damaging rooms on the Bras Basah Road side.

The first fatalities were recorded on 12 April 1964, when a bomb exploded on the ground floor of a nearly-completed block of HDB flats just off Changi Road. Chunks of concrete

Historic Katong Park

This lovely little park was recognised as a historic site in 1998 by the National Heritage Board. Its plaque notes that the 1963 bomb here 'marked the beginning of Konfrontasi (Confrontation) when Indonesia, led by Sukarno, opposed the formation of Malaysia which, until 1965, included Singapore. Within two weeks, two more bombs went off here. There was no casualties in all three incidents'.

smashed into a nearby wooden house, killing two occupants and injuring six others.

In February 1965, 24 Indonesians approaching the southwestern tip of Johor (near Pulau Kukup) in two boats with what was described as 'a considerable quantity of arms and ammunition' were intercepted by a Royal Malaysian Navy patrol boat. One boat with 10 men was easily captured, the other put up a fight which resulted in one of the Indonesians being shot dead.

On 1 April 1965, a bomb placed inside a Morris Oxford car exploded in the ground-floor carpark of the old Odeon cinema (now Odeon Tower) on North Bridge Road, damaging four other cars. On 8 July, 22 Indonesian-made hand grenades were found at three different locations after phone tip-offs: in a temporary carpark next to the CID building on Robinson Road; in a phone booth on River Valley Road by the now-gone St Nicholas flats; and just outside Newton Post office at Newton Circus.

Like most of the preceding bombs, these proved to have nuisance value only, aiming to create an atmosphere of uncertainty and fear. None would have so much of an impact or so high a casualty list as that one at MacDonald House ...

A Dream of 'Mahamalaya'

What had led Indonesia to declare its pointless guerilla war on 'Greater' Malaysia in 1963? For the answer, the personality of independent Indonesia's first president, Achmed Sukarno, must be considered – as must Japan's proposed altering of the Southeast Asia political map following its 1942 conquest of the region.

Japan intended to 'allow' three independent nations – Burma, the Philippines, and a new Annam Empire based on Cambodia. Japan then wanted a series of 'protected' states that included Laos, the then Dutch East Indies island of Java and a new national concept that unified the island of Sumatra and British Malaya (which would then lose four of its northern sultanates – Kedah, Perlis, Kelantan and Terengganu – to Thailand).

Singapore and Penang, plus some other strategic naval bases, would (like Hong Kong) become out-and-out Japanese colonies. Then, immediately after the Japanese surrender, the radical new Malay Nationalist Party (which regarded the newly-formed UMNO as too elitist in nature) campaigned to take Malaya into an independent Indonesia.

When Sukarno came to power in 1950, all this – especially that plan to detach Sumatra – weighed on his mind. For, in his view, Malaya's ruling sultans and aristocracy had failed to take an open stand against Japan's wartime advance precisely because they had been promised this plus-Sumatra national extension, which would have created a new nation under the ungainly name of 'Mahamalaya'.

General Count Terauchi himself, Japan's Supreme Commander in Southeast Asia (who now lies buried in the Chuan Hoe Avenue Japanese cemetery), chaired the meeting in Ipoh that was intended to launch this state of 'Mahamalaya' – with its historical and racial 'justification' of inheriting the ancient Sumatran Buddhist empire of Srivijaya (11th–13th centuries). Java-born Sukarno had not forgotten this intended pre-independence 'dismemberment' as among other things, Sumatra's considerable mineral wealth (oil, mainly) was of crucial economic importance to the new Indonesia.

Then Britain, seeking a lasting post-colonial settlement, decided in 1963 to include within the new Federation of Malaysia its former protectorates in north Borneo – Sarawak and Sabah (oil-rich Brunei opting for independence) – thus creating a land border with which Indonesia was uncomfortable on the island it knew as Kalimantan. Sukarno's short-fuse patience exploded.

For he saw himself as Big Cheese in this corner of Southeast Asia, what with Indonesia's huge population, and his instincts towards the Third World concept of 'newly-emerging nations' which left him susceptible to provocative promptings from both Moscow and Peking. For Sukarno, Jakarta would be the regional capital; not Kuala Lumpur, not Singapore, not anywhere in the British-inspired, British-protected, neo-colonial and capitalistic Malaysia.

Sukarno's 'A-Bomb'

The potential global communist dimension and threat of the Konfrontasi was indicated by the attendance at a June 1964 Jakarta mass rally of Mr Anastas Mikoyan, then the Soviet First Deputy Prime Minister. He publicly stated that the USSR was ready to send President Sukarno 'modern weapons, far better than the British possess in this area' to help Indonesia's bid to 'crush' Malaysia.

And in June 1965, at a Muslim conference in Bandung, Sukarno declared that Indonesia would soon produce its own A-bomb to 'maintain the country's territorial integrity from outside interference'. As with so many of Sukarno's later utterances, this atomic threat turned out to be mere bluster ...

Sukarno's crude response was to declare his intention to 'crush' this new Malaysia, and his campaign started off with incursions across the border between those two 'stolen' Borneo states and Indonesian Kalimantan, and into Brunei. Some 6,000 Indonesian volunteers were pumped into the fray of a raging rebellion there, with Sukarno hoping that a contrary Brunei might serve as a wedge between the two new Malaysian states. This rebellion flopped, so Sukarno turned his attention to Malaysia itself. On 20 January 1963, the Konfrontasi was officially declared.

Its first consequences were witnessed in Sarawak's jungles, but British and Malaysian counter-terrorist forces successfully flushed out these infiltrators (mainly Chinese and communist-inspired), rendering them ineffectual by the end of the year.

The first consequences ...

In Singapore itself, the damage was done by a 300-strong group made up of Indonesian agents, Chinese left-wingers and Malay extremists who had been trained (ironically) on Sumatra in the 'arts' of sabotage and terrorism, then slipped into Singapore on barter boats with their arms and explosives hidden in sacks of charcoal and copra.

Sukarno did not get his way, of course. Even the forced departure of Singapore on 9 August 1965 from the Malaysian Federation was neither his doing nor his desire. And on 4 August 1966, Indonesia's Information Minister Mr Burhanuddin Diah told reporters in Jakarta that the Konfrontasi would be formally buried by that month's National Day (17 August).

Bloodbath in Indonesia

It was Sukarno himself who felt the backlash caused by his failure to 'crush' Malaysia. It came in the wake of the alleged PKI coup launched on 30 September 1965, with the assassination of six senior army generals whose mutilated bodies were dumped down a disused well in East Jakarta, now known as the Lubang Buaya (crocodile hole) Monument. Six months later, up to half-a-million (mainly Chinese) PKI members had been killed in a vicious bloodbath conducted by Indonesia's army and fanatic Muslim groups. The PKI has remained strictly illegal ever since.

The then Army Minister Major-General Suharto took over as Indonesia's leader on 12 March 1967. Sukarno – the 'Father of the Nation' – was allowed to save face by *A new leader emerges ...* keeping the title of President for a further 12 months before being finally put out to pasture. Continued purges obliterated remaining Sukarno supporters in the army and left-leaning influential political figures, as Suharto's New Order government achieved the near-permanent ruling status it held until suddenly in May 1998 ...

Bung Karno (as he was affectionately known by many) died in 1970, and for eight years laid buried in a small unmarked grave beside his Balinese mother at Blitar in southern East Java. Then in 1978, for internal political reasons, Suharto authorised the removal of Sukarno's remains (and those of his parents) to

Chinese Agony

In the bloody riots that raged through Indonesia's cities throughout 1998, it was the Chinese community – rich and poor – who suffered the brunt of the pain (which in May saw Suharto finally forced to release his reins of power, after 32 years of unchallenged power).

Particularly distressing were the many Chinese women (officially said to number 66, though some say more) who were raped during the May riots. Indonesia's new rulers realise it will take time and care to restore a proper and humane relationship with its economically-crucial Chinese community.

a specially-built grand marble mausoleum just outside off-the-beaten-track Blitar. This now goes under the name Sentul, the 'Grave of the Declarer of Indonesia's Independence', and attracts many visitors. Sukarno was born in East Java's capital city of Surabaya but he'd asked to be buried close to his parents (who had lived in Blitar).

The primarily Chinese flavouring of the PKI resulted in Suharto refusing to re-open full diplomatic ties with China until 1990, 23 years after Jakarta had formally accused Beijing of involvement with that 1965 coup. There are now some 6 million ethnic Chinese among Indonesia's total 200 million population, controlling up to 60 percent of the nation's wealth.

But it's only a handful who are among the nation's super-rich. The vast majority continue to live modestly, even subdued, with a lingering hint of 'suspicion' over their heads. Some examples: Chinese languages or characters are not allowed in public, Lunar New Year cards are discouraged, Chinese people are 'encouraged' to render their names Indonesian, etc.

Only in August 1994 was the total ban on Chinese lettering lifted, and then solely for the purposes of encouraging tourism from China. Announcing this mild easing-up, Armed Forces Chief General Feisal Tanjung said there was still a need 'to be cautious about the past' (i.e. that 1965 coup).

As for Indonesia-Malaysia relations, some underlying tension remains despite the generally close Asean-inspired links. At the back of it lies that disputed Big Brother slot – Indonesia with its huge population or Malaysia with its more advanced economic development?

For its part, Singapore took its own post-Konfrontasi steps by introducing compulsory National Service that meant (and still means) all young men turning 18 must spend at least two years in 'Army Daze' **Army daze ...** training. Just in case, as the example of Kuwait's invasion by its far more powerful neighbour Iraq demonstrated in August 1990.

Who was MacDonald?

Malcolm MacDonald was not – as some football buffs might suspect – the former noted Arsenal, Newcastle and England centre-forward, but the rather appealing British Governor-General for Southeast Asia from 1948–55. Appealing because he was an unstuffy and unconventional colonial administrator who, for instance, hated going to the Tanglin Club because of its then whites-only policy.

In 1954, UK newspaper *The Daily Express* reacted strongly when it saw a photo showing MacDonald in Sarawak happily in-between two pretty and very bare-breasted (as was their wont) Dayak women. The paper thundered this was 'beyond the limit' and that his preoccupation seemed to be 'to set Malaya on the Indian path out of the Empire'.

The anti-colonialist *Daily Mirror* however praised MacDonald's easy-going ways such as his dislike for 'the tyranny of the dinner jacket', with the paper saying he'd delivered 'a sartorial face-slap to the snob clubs of Singapore'.

MacDonald House today goes about its normal business as if nothing untowards ever happened there. But something most certainly untowards did happen, something the likes of which all would hope never does happen again ...

The First Skyscraper in Town

Cathay Building
11 Dhoby Ghaut

*Opened in 1939, Cathay Building became the
springboard for Datuk Loke Wan Tho's movie empire ...*

The handsome Cathay Building has become such a familiar Singapore landmark, it feels like it's been there for ever. In local terms, it has. It was opened in 1939 as the first 'skyscraper' in town and enjoyed an unbroken run of 15 years as Singapore's biggest building.

Just imagine how the building must have struck people when it first appeared. For the visual scene around Dhoby Ghaut was then a tranquil one. Nearby stood the old-style YMCA while opposite was the serene, highly European, Ladies Lawn Tennis Club (which figured in Noel Barber's *Tanamera* potboiler) on what is now Bras Basah Park.

Author, Author

An image of Cathay Building served as the company's corporate logo until 1965. The building proved a lasting image for visitors, too. When British dramatist Peter Nichols (*Privates on Parade*, *Poppy*, etc) arrived here in mid-1994 as NIE's first playwright-in-residence, he recalled late-1940s' Singapore (he was here on RAF service) thus: 'It was like any Eastern town and the tallest building was the Cathay Building.'

Another British writer fond of the Cathay was Leslie Thomas, who made his name with *Virgin Soldiers*. This novel's main female character was a Chinese call-girl named Juicy Lucy, based on a movie-loving cabaret girl he befriended while on army service here in 1950–51 and whom he took every week to Cathay cinema. Thomas recalled: 'She used to bring her whole family, including her grandparents, nieces and nephews, along on our dates at the Cathay.'

On the Cathay site, Louis Molteri's popular bakery and confectioner had stood since the 1880s until its demolition in 1934. The land thus vacated was bought up by the Loke family, with its ambitious plans for setting up a Singapore base for the movie-theatre operation it had launched in 1935 under the name Associate Theatres.

Construction work started at Dhoby Ghaut in 1937. One million dollars and two years later, the entertainment complex was ready to dazzle Singaporeans. In an era when the irksome phrase 'one-stop shop' did not exist, this was just that. **A one-stop shop ...** According to family scion Datuk Loke Wan Tho (son of Malayan rubber magnate Loke Yew), the Cathay complex would be where locals could 'go to shop, have their hair done, have a meal, see a show, and then go to the cabaret at night'. The first movie its 1,300-seat cinema screened (on 3 October 1939) was Korda's Sudan adventure yarn *The Four Feathers*.

Above and behind this huge cinema soared the 17-storey Cathay Building, reaching 83.5 m to the tip of its distinctive water tower. This building was Singapore's only 'skyscraper' until the handsome Asia Insurance Building arose from Finlayson Green in 1954.

War Moves in on Cathay

The Cathay complex did not enjoy peaceful civilian status for long. In 1941, many of its storeys were taken over by the British military administration as war loomed ever closer. The cinema kept going, even when victorious Japanese officers moved into the building. Indeed, at their insistence, the latest patriotic movies from Tokyo were screened twice a day. And after the Japanese had moved out again, Cathay cinema celebrated with a special screening of Allied war movie *Desert Victory*.

Admiral Lord Louis Mountbatten was Supreme Allied Commander in Southeast Asia. After accepting the Japanese surrender at City Hall on 12 September 1945, he set his HQ up in Cathay Building (he was there for a year). There's a plaque from Lord Mountbatten, presented in thanks to Mrs Loke Yew, up in the lobby entrance on the Mount Sophia side.

The Golden Age of Cathay

Post-war, Datuk Loke set about striking deals with such foreign film giants as Rank, MGM, 20th Century Fox and Columbia that would bring blockbuster first-run movies to Cathay, keeping it one step ahead of the rival Shaw Brothers and its Lido and Capitol cinemas. He achieved the quantity too, with over 60 cinema theatres around Singapore and Malaya by the 1950s.

Mountbatten: The Man, The Controversy

In Singapore, Mountbatten has also left his name to a major road, a constituency and more. But in recent times, British 'Young Turk' historians have subjected his reputation to critical scrutiny – and revision.

One such insisted that Mountbatten had from the 1930s onwards been 'promoted wildly above his abilities, with consistently disastrous consequences'. While in Singapore, the ('largely spiritual') relationship Mountbatten's wife Edwina was said to have enjoyed with Pandit Nehru was put forward as one reason why Mountbatten proceeded 'with indecent haste' in his partition of India, cutting through Punjab and creating Pakistan (at midnight on 14 August 1947).

The one million-odd deaths in the population transfers this 'rushed' partition provoked led British historian Andrew Roberts to insist that Mountbatten actually 'should have been impeached', rather than claiming himself a secure and favourable place in British decolonialisation history. Mountbatten was killed by an IRA bomb while sailing off the west coast of Ireland in 1979.

In 1953, Datuk Loke went one step further. He teamed up with Mr Ho Ah Loke to establish a movie-making studio titled Cathay-Keris Films, off Tampines Road. Movie number one from this new enterprise was *Buloh Perindu*, the first all-colour Malay language film made in Singapore.

Soon there was a regular production line of mainly Malay full-length feature movies coming out of Cathay-Keris Studio each year. The *Pontianak* series was a noted success, but more so were those starring that giant of the Malay movie world – P. Ramlee, actor, director, singer and more. In all, some 120 movies emerged from Cathay-Keris before its demise in 1968.

In 1955, Datuk Loke had gone another step further, by buying Hong Kong's ailing Yonghua Studio and financing a vibrant Chinese movie-making industry to feed his cinema chain. His first Chinese **A step further ..** hit was the 1957 flirty-funny musical *Mambo Girl* (its top song was *I Love Cha Cha*), starring Grace Chang. Grace thereby became the first in Cathay's stable of Chinese movie stars – with Lin Dai, Yu Min, Chang Yang, Julie Yeh Fung, Jeanette Lin Tsui and more to follow. Their movies were a strong and glamorous mix of musicals, comedies, romances and dramas.

They often achieved critical acclaim as well as commercial success, with Linda Lin Dai winning the Best Actress Award in 1957 for her part in *Golden Lotus* at the 4th Asian Film Festival in Tokyo ('Unforgettable' Lin Dai would commit suicide in 1964, aged 29). The next year, with the film fest in Manila, the comedy-drama *Our Sister Hedy* (its Chinese title translated as *Four Daughters*, played by Soo Fung, Lin Tsui, Yeh Fung and Mu Hung) was named Best Picture. In 1959, Lucilla Yu Ming won Best Actress for *Her Tender Heart* (she won again in 1960, for *All in the Family*).

Once Upon a Time in Cathay Hotel

In 1954, three of the floors above the cinema (which had been occupied by Radio Malaya) were opened up as the Cathay Hotel, soon enlarged to contain 165 air-con rooms and to gain a high reputation for the Chinese food and the 'lavish international floor shows' in its Cathay Restaurant and Nightclub.

This hotel operation ceased in 1970 when a surge of modern hotel building programme left Cathay's building limping behind in the comfort stakes. The hotel rooms were switched back to offices and in 1978 the outside of the building also took on a different shape as the balconies and alcoves that had given it an almost-Mediterranean look were filled in and covered by a curtain wall to take on its current external visuals.

With the competitive movie-making heat rising from Shaw (which had its Singapore movie studio at Jalan Ampas, off Balestier Road), Cathay produced what is still regarded as its best-ever picture – *Sun, Moon & Star* (1960). It struck another crowd-pleaser in 1961 with *The Greatest Civil War on Earth*, combining Mandarin and Cantonese with an engaging north versus south China 'family duel' as its theme. Cathay's Hong Kong movie-making arm closed down in 1970, with over 200 films to its credit. It had actually began running out of steam following Datuk Loke's tragic death in 1964 as his creative flair and bubbling enthusiasm for movie-making was a major factor in its successes.

Tragedy and New Directions

In 1964, tragedy struck Cathay. Datuk Loke, his wife Mavis and other Cathay Organisation executives were killed in an internal air crash while attending the 11th Asian Film Festival in Taiwan. His sister, Lady Yuen Peng McNiece, took over the business.

A Capitol Cinema

Capitol Theatre, the last old-style big cinema in the Shaw Brothers chain that rivals Cathay, was shut down in December 1998. But fret not, the wrecker's ball will not flatten this art deco delight. Now a government building, it will probably re-emerge as a London West End-style venue for musical and theatre shows.

Built in 1929, it was renamed Kyoei Gekkyo by the occupying Japanese (who renamed Cathay Cinema as Dai Tao Gekkyo) and screened only Japanese and propaganda movies till it was hit in 1944 by a bomb planted by 'anti-Japanese elements'. Post-war, Shaw Organisation bought the complex for $3 million as its flagship cinema (it could seat 1,690). Many Singaporeans of a certain age recall the rendezvous message: 'See you at the Capitol lobby'. While inside, like the old Lido, many couples enjoyed their first dates.

In 1965, the 1,118-seat $6 million Orchard Cinema-cum-bowling alley just off Orchard Road by Mandarin Hotel was opened. In 1971 at Jurong, Cathay launched the region's first drive-in cinema. The opening film on the giant 14.3 x 33.5 m screen (some 7.6 m above the ground and tilted at an angle of six-and-a-half degrees) was a limp British comedy called *Doctor in Trouble*. The drive-in settled into a good run, with its Bruce Lee movie screenings especially popular, until September 1985 (well into the home video age) when dismal audiences made it pointless. Its site is now covered by Tang Dynasty City.

In 1990, a posh 350-seat arthouse cinema called The Picturehouse opened to screen 'commercially non-viable' serious stuff (plus Restricted-A category naughties) for brain-starved local movie buffs. In October 1994, Cathay's Orchard Theatre was shut down to become the $50 million nine-storey, five-cinema plus-plus entertainment complex called Orchard Cineleisure.

New Movie Moves

In 1995, Cathay set up a new film-making subsidiary called Cathay Asia Films, which has so far concentrated on small-scale local films such as *Army Daze* (1996), *The Teenage Textbook Movie* (1998) and the $800,000 Jack Neo vehicle *That One No Enough* (1999). It has also invested in overseas productions such as Tsui Hark's animated Hong Kong film, *A Chinese Ghost Story*.

Cathay knows that respect and feel-good sentiment, derived from how it so boldly erected such a landmark building on Dhoby Ghaut, will alone not see it through into the 21st century.

The Curry Murder

Presbyterian church caretaker's house
Penang Road

*An Indian caretaker is clubbed to death,
chopped up into little pieces and cooked
with rice and spices ...*

The historic Presbyterian church by the bus-stop on Penang Road (where it curves off from Orchard Road for Park Mall) is rightly guarded by the Protection of Monuments Board. A complex is attached to this church, including a little caretaker's house at the back which looks sweet.

Sweet – and such an unlikely setting for a 1984 murder that upon its belated discovery three years later got the world's news agency wires buzzing, directing international attention towards what was soon known as the 'Curry Murder Horror'.

It was a murder for which no body (or, more accurately, body parts) was found, no murder weapon unearthed and, in the end, for which nobody was convicted – though six people did appear before a judge in June 1987. This gory story began in December 1984. Then, Mr Ayakanno Marimuthu, a 38-year-old caretaker, was reported missing from his home at the PUB chalets on Biggin Hill Road, Changi. His 32-year-old wife reported his absence at the Joo Chiat police station, saying that her husband had told her he was off to Genting Highlands and its roulette wheels. He had not returned home.

The police file was left open on the case, with Mr Marimuthu officially registered as a missing person. Eventually his apparently-abandoned wife took their three children with her to the Foochew Methodist Church on Race Course Road, where she started work as a caretaker.

Two years on, in January 1987, Detective V. Alagamalai received a tip-off in a hawker centre from a long-standing, well-trusted contact. What it alleged was extremely difficult for the experienced policeman to accept.

He said: 'I was disgusted and couldn't believe that what he was telling me was the truth then. I listened with disbelief as he told me that three men had killed an Indian caretaker in an Orchard Road church in 1984 and had disposed of the body by chopping it up and cooking it with curry and rice.'

Rounding Up Suspects

Detective Alagamalai was initially unable to get his superiors to believe the shocking story. Assistant Superintendent Cheok Koon Seng remarked: 'It was difficult to believe that this could happen in modern-day Singapore.' Nonetheless, the detective investigated further and soon decided the Genting Highlands 'alibi' story was unlikely. He also learned that the missing man was a wife-beater with a vicious temper when inflamed by alcohol. By March he had gathered in enough new information to get a 'carry on' nod from his superiors.

A wife-beater with a vicious temper ...

He had three suspects in mind. One of them was a mutton butcher at a Commonwealth Avenue wet market stall. The detective felt this might fit the picture, as a heavy butcher's chopper (and technique) would have been needed to cut the victim's body into small pieces.

On 23 March 1987 at 2 am, police teams swooped on five different addresses, including the Orchard Road church, and roped in eight suspects. At first, all eight kept quiet on the subject of the 'vanished' Mr Marimuthu.

Then, two days later, one of the suspects did sing, alleging that the victim had been clubbed to death with an iron bar in the Presbyterian church's caretaker quarters. Then the extraordinary 'cover-up' details emerged: in the old kitchen within the caretaker's lodge, Mr Marimuthu was then chopped up into little pieces and cooked with rice and spices in a large aluminium pot of the kind used in Indian eateries to make *nasi briyani*.

CID director Jagjit Singh commented: 'This is one of the most unusual and bizarre murder cases handled by police – unusual because the remains of the body have never been found … bizarre because of the manner in which the body was disposed of.'

When the charges were made public, the Penang Road Presbyterian church's business manager, Mr Symen Gjaltema, responded in shocked disbelief: 'Oh no … surely you are kidding … It's terrible … something very sad and very unfortunate.'

Mr Gjaltema said the caretaker's premises had been renovated the year before (1986) and that the kitchen, where he now knew a grisly murder took place, had been modernised from its 'very primitive state … with an old-fashioned portable stove and a makeshift sink'. He agreed that the disappeared-now-deceased victim had a 'hot temper' but said he would soon calm down again. He described Mr Marimuthu's extended family unit as appearing to be 'closely-knit'.

Mystery of the Remains

So, what did happen to the victim's 'curried' remains? It seems that his cooked flesh and body parts, including cracked pieces of skull and bones, were packed into black bin-liner plastic bags and dumped into various roadside rubbish bins. No suspicion had been aroused this way. The remains of Mr Marimuthu had simply been taken away as if they really were the leftover food they were cooked to resemble.

History Happens

The whole Orchard Road Presbyterian church complex is now a registered historic site. It was set up in 1875, following on from the original Presbyterian ministry started in Singapore by Scotland's Mackenzie Fraser in 1856.

On 27 March 1987, Mrs Naragatha Vally Ramiah, the seemingly abandoned wife, and three of her brothers (including the caretaker of the Presbyterian church and the meat butcher) appeared in court to face murder charges. Later, two others faced charges of aiding and abetting the murder. They were the widow's mother and her sister-in-law.

On 6 June, they were all released for 'lack of proof', which fell short of an actual acquittal. The three brothers were immediately re-arrested and held under the Criminal Law (Temporary Provisions) Act. They were detained until June 1991, when they were released unconditionally from Changi prison. Their first act, as with other inmates upon release, was to go to Changi beach, strip off their clothes and swim in the sea to 'cleanse' themselves. Then followed a happy family reunion in Ang Mo Kio.

All six involved people are still anxious that the Singapore High Court gives them a complete acquittal to remove a lingering suspicion of doubt over a murder they insist they did not commit. For their part, the police regard the Marimuthu case as a still-unsolved murder.

In 1996, the six released people failed in a legal action alleging defamation by *The Straits Times*, which they alleged had suggested that they were responsible for the curry murder. The paper had written up a report on a TCS proposal to dramatise the curry murder over five episodes of a Mandarin drama series.

Even today, it is difficult for those who know the full 'Curry Murder Horror' story details to pass the Presbyterian church's little caretaker lodge without a little shudder ...

The Tiger of France

Clemenceau Avenue

Sharp-witted and sharp-tongued, Georges
Clemenceau was a toppler of ministers, idol of
Singapore, 'father of 123 children' ...

'America is the only nation in history which mericulously
has gone directly from barbarism to degeneracy without
the usual interval of civilisation.'

That's the perky 1929 soundbite for which many still know
Georges Clemenceau. In Singapore, his name is better known
because of that busy avenue that runs alongside the CTE road
tunnel and across Orchard Road.

This avenue took its name from Clemenceau during his
visit to Singapore in November 1920, when he attended the
foundation stone laying ceremony for the Esplanade's Memorial
(dedicated to the 124 Singaporeans who lost their lives in
Europe's World War I, and formally unveiled in March 1922).
Since Clemenceau was in town and since he was still such a
huge political figure, he was also invited to 'turn the first sod'
for a new road that would be finished by 1925 – and speedily
named Clemenceau Avenue in his honour.

As a real colossus, Clemenceau had paced the French
political stage from 1906–January 1920 but his tour of the Far
East was made as a 79-year-old ex-politician, one forced much
against his will into retirement.

He had served his first term as France's Prime Minister from
1906–1910. Then, as a major critic of French bungling in the
early years of World War I, he was made Premier again – plus
Minister for War – in 1917. It was his inspiration that kept
French spirits alive till the tide of war turned in 1918, earning
him the popular tag 'Tiger of France'.

A Towering Figure in Versailles

At the 1919 peace treaty negotiations in Versailles's Hall of Mirrors near Paris, it was Clemenceau who towered over the other European figures. When the 180-strong delegation representing defeated Germany turned up (in a train ordered to move at a slow 10 mph so that the Germans could witness the damage their armies had caused), Clemenceau produced another stirring soundbite: 'The hour has struck for the weighty settlement of our account.'

Yet the French premier was damned by his compatriots – and by the US – for being too lenient to Germany. For despite his deep anger at the horrendous human losses induced by German declaration of war in 1914, he'd warned against placing too heavy a burden on the Germans. French resentment was such that Clemenceau was squeezed out of office before the end of 1919. Take note, just before he died in 1929, he made a chilling prediction. That

A chilling prediction ...

Germany's resurgence and desire for revenge would provoke another savage world war – in 1940. He was out by only months.

In 1920, Clemenceau was thus a newly-discarded politician. Yet far from being bitter, he was in perky spirits. He certainly enjoyed his week-long stay here, according to the account given by Singapore's then Governor Sir Lawrence Guillemard in the London newspaper *The Times*: 'The charm of his manner was irresistible; his gay humour was infectious; his courtesy won all hearts, and in two days he was the idol of Singapore.'

Clemenceau stayed at Government House (today's Istana) and insisted every morning on having porridge (of the oats variety), despite the customary French horror at this unsubtle dish. He insisted to his surprised manservant: 'I am on English soil, and so I will eat an English breakfast.'

Guillemard passed on some regional advice to his guest. Clemenceau's next stop was Java and he was warned about 'a native Rajah' there who would ask him how many children he had, and who would then easily trump that figure by insisting he himself had produced 85. Thus forewarned, Clemenceau reported on his way back through Singapore that he had claimed 123 children when asked this 'how many?' question. The stunned Rajah, he claimed, had 'no spirit left in him'!

Clemenceau had been known from the earliest stages of his political career (he narrowly escaped death in the 1871 Paris Commune) as a man with a sharp tongue. Through the effectiveness of the vicious verbal rapier he used against government members he regarded as incompetents, he also became known in France as the 'Toppler of Ministers'.

But what, recalling that 'barbarism to degeneracy' remark, did Clemenceau have against the US? Maybe because as a young man, Clemenceau had rashly married an American woman? This had broken up unhappily, leaving him a misanthrope as well as stuck with decidedly negative views towards Americans.

At least this sharp-witted, sharp-tongued French statesman would be happy to know his Clemenceau Avenue is so busy these days – and not at all a side-alley, like the political one into which he had been pushed just a few months before he visited Singapore ...

Eastwards Towards Geylang

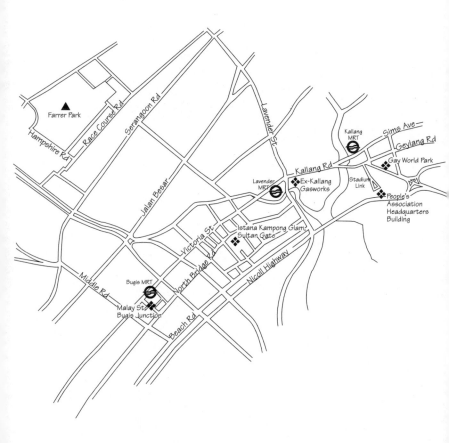

Not Just a Playing Field

Farrer Park
Hampshire Road

*When horses and airplanes converged on
Singapore's first racing course ...*

It was just short of Singapore's 25th anniversary when its
British residents realised there was something seriously
absent from this tropical island: a horse-racing course. This
was deemed such an urgent priority that much effort and
expense went into draining and de-jungling a patch of swamp
to create what is known today as Farrer Park.

Soon here appeared white rails, well-tended lawns and
tracks and all the race-course paraphernalia to soothe that
English nostalgic yearning. Not forgetting a small but dignified
grandstand to hold the white elite (though soon more
grandstand space would be required for prominent local
towkays and the Sultan of Johor's party).

On 23 February 1843, the starter's flag went up on the
island's first organised horse-race – the Singapore Cup, with
prize money of $150 and amateur jockey-owners riding
Javanese ponies. Half the island, it seems, turned up for this
big race which was won, incidentally, by William Read on his
mount called Colonel.

Before long, Farrer Park race meets were a crucial part of
the island's social life. On Governor's Cup Day, a mini-Epsom
Derby Day atmosphere was recreated just north of the Equator,
with the Governor and his good lady wife being driven across
the lawns to the grandstand, accompanied by the Johor military
band playing the British national anthem. And after the races,
the frock coats and sun parasols in the grandstand would
transfer to Government House (today's Istana) for the grandest
of Singapore's grand balls.

It was at Farrer Park also that organised golf took off in Singapore, with a nine-hole course opening up in the middle of the racetrack in 1891. Not to mention polo (and occasional rifle-shooting practice). Soon there would be bitter rows with the Polo Club over the use of the race course on non-racing days. Golf finally triumphed in 1913 when the Polo Club moved first to Balestier, before taking up its current home off Thomson Road in 1947.

No sports whatsoever could take place after heavy rain, for tropical downpours would turn the park into a two m-deep lake with the rainwater often lapping over the white racing rails. This also made the park an unhealthy zone, and thus an unfortunate choice for the location of the Kandang Kerbau hospital on part of the race course grounds in 1860, together with a lunatic asylum. These 'temples of medicine' were hit in 1873 by a cholera epidemic, worsened by the unhealthy (i.e. dirty water) park conditions and by overcrowding.

A Flying Start

There's more to Farrer Park's early history than sports and sickness. For on 16 March 1911, the first airplane flight in Singapore took off from its race course. At the controls was a Frenchman (Joseph Christiaens) who had conveyed his device here in kit-form by ship, aiming to give a three-day display of aviation wonders – just eight years after the Wright brothers' first-ever flight. The Royal Engineers helped him assemble his Bristol Box-Kite biplane, powered by its 50 hp Gnome engine allegedly capable of pushing the lightweight plane to a speed of 40 mph.

Monsieur Christiaens was soon having problems with local conditions. All he could manage at first was 60 metres above the race course and, with invited passengers on board, just six metres up as they flew gracefully over the race circuit. On the third day, he got his plane up to 150 metres near Bukit Timah, after dropping a pretend 'bomb' on the race course's golf links.

Singapore had thus witnessed its first manned flights, though to go by press reports of the time, nobody was that excited by it. World War I with its daring 'Red Baron' aerial duels and such like would change public attitudes towards planes, even in distant Singapore.

Touchdown on the Course

Especially when at approximately 4.48 pm on Thursday, 4 December 1919, a Vickers Vimy touched down on the race course. For this plane, the first to land on Singaporean soil (Christiaens had arrived by sea), had come a long way. Some 13,900 km. It had taken off from Hounslow in west London 22 days before and stopped in France, Italy, Crete, Egypt, Syria, Karachi, **An epic flight ...** India, Burma and Thailand before touching down on Singapore's race course. Its ultimate destination was Darwin in Australia's Northern Territory and the $10,000 prize that was on offer for the first Australians to fly the 17,900 km from Britain in under 30 days.

Piloted by two brothers (Captain Ross Smith and Lt Keith Smith, assisted by Sgts Jim Bennett and Wally Shiers), it reached its target successfully. Their epic flight is now commemorated by the Ross Smith Memorial obelisk, just outside Darwin.

Their arrival at Singapore's race course was described thus by *The Straits Times*: 'Coming over the east end, the machine flew the whole length of the ground, affording a splendid view to everybody. Then, making a complete circle, it flew far away to the south. Returning, it passed over the west end, gradually descending, and made a splendid landing in the middle of the course.'

This news report may have missed the real reason for such a cautious approach, which was not simply to thrill the crowds. The race course was the smallest of the 'temporary aerodromes' the plane had encountered on its voyage, so it had to approach most cautiously, then be slowed down drastically upon landing.

This effect was achieved in a uniquely dashing way by Sgt Bennett. He climbed out of his rear cockpit as soon as the plane's wheels hit the ground and slid down the plane's tail so his bodyweight slowed it down. This makeshift plan worked, and the plane shuddered to a final halt after taxi-ing just 90 metres along the race track. This 'human anchor' method of slowing a landing plane down to a halt is not often witnessed these days on Changi airport runways ...

God 'Elp All Of Us ...

Thousands of spectators greeted the visitors. One of their voices was heard to ask what the 'G-EA-OU' initials along the plane's fuselage stood for. Ross Smith allegedly replied: 'God 'Elp All Of Us'. It was, of course, really the plane's registration code, with the 'G' standing for Great Britain.

In Darwin, the historic flight was further hailed for bringing closer 'the day when, by a chain of permanent stations, the aerial post between England and Australia will be an accomplished fact.' It was not until 1926 that this route was commercially scouted by Britain's Imperial Airways (by seaplane). And it was not until 1929 that Singapore's first proper airport (as opposed to race track) was opened at Seletar.

Not before time. For in 1927, when the American millionaire playboy W. van Lear Black touched down on the

Horses Go Places

Singapore's race course is on the gallop again. The Bukit Timah site is being sold off for redevelopment and the new turf club at Kranji should open in 1999 by staging the Singapore International Cup – the sixth richest horse race in the world, with top prize of $3 million.

swampy Balestier Plain in his Fokker monoplane (chartered from KLM), *The Straits Times* was livid. The Fokker had to be flown the short distance across to the race course with just its pilot on board. Only that way could it take off again with its full complement and reach its final destination of Batavia (today's Jakarta), thus giving the Dutch a headstart over Britain on the Southeast Asia air route.

The newspaper noted: 'All this is no credit to Singapore, and it is not very pleasant to have to listen to aerial visitors making caustic comparisons between the lack of facilities here and the well-equipped aerodrome provided by the Siamese close to Bangkok.'

Meanwhile, what of the race course? In February 1919, it was the scene of Centenary Day celebrations when thousands packed the grounds to rejoice. During the 1920s, more and more buildings impinged upon the track until in 1933, the horses quit. In 1934, the Singapore Turf Club moved to the splendid ex-rubber estate 140-acre site off Bukit Timah Road it occupies today.

Farrer Park's horses are these days recalled only by the street name Race Course Road, a strip now so distinguished for its Indian eateries that it's informally known as 'curry row'. That old race course grandstand disappeared under a food centre and the early public housing that line the road. And the race course was renamed Farrer Park.

But Farrer Park's historical significance was not yet done. There was still the Occupation to come ...

Loyalty Above All

On 17 February 1942, two days after the British surrender, Indian and Malay PoW soldiers were assembled on Farrer Park and urged to switch their fighting loyalty to Japan. Eight Malay officers refused. They were promptly taken away for execution, along with 100 of their men, all heroic (and ferocious) fighters from the Malay Regiment's final stand at Pasir Panjang.

The Indian soldiers were given the choice of wartime imprisonment or joining the newly-formed Indian National Army, military wing of the Indian Independence League run by the charismatic ex-President of the Indian Congress, Subash Chandra Bose. Bose would on 24 October 1943 pull a massive Indian crowd to the Padang, just three days after declaring himself prime minister of the 'Provisional Government of Free India' which was quickly officially recognised by Japan and which thus quickly declared war on Britain and the US.

In Singapore, the INA was organised by one Rash Behari Bose and headquartered at the erstwhile Anzac Club on Waterloo Street. The purpose of both these bodies was to exploit the Japan-Britain war for its own ends: independence for India. It had the battle-cry of 'Let us go to Delhi!'

The INA first saw action on the Burma front in 1944 but made little impression, even if it did briefly manage to raise its flag on Indian soil. The British advance, plus large-scale desertion from its own ranks, soon rendered the INA impotent.

In May 1945, Subhas Chandra Bose came back to Singapore and set up his headquarters in Katong. But Bose was killed in a still-mysterious air crash in Taiwan that August, just before the Japanese surrender saw the final dissolving (and removal of a small INA memorial from the Padang) of both the INA

Indonesian PoWs

Also in those early Occupation days of 1942, thousands of Indonesian prisoners were brought to Singapore on their way to forced resettlement in Sumatra. They were 'housed' on Farrer Park, but their rations soon ran out and many died on the old race course of malnutrition, dysentery or typhoid. Many also quietly slipped away and merged into the Malay community, becoming Singaporean citizens after 1945.

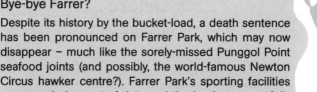

Bye-bye Farrer?

Despite its history by the bucket-load, a death sentence has been pronounced on Farrer Park, which may now disappear – much like the sorely-missed Punggol Point seafood joints (and possibly, the world-famous Newton Circus hawker centre?). Farrer Park's sporting facilities are regarded as out-of-date and the land more usefully used for redevelopment.

and its 'Provisional Government'. The political initiative in India went back to the Indian National Congress, which in 1941 had decisively broken with the INA's controversial stance.

The Occupation over, Farrer Park hosted another major event on 12 September 1946. Then, 20,000 mainly Chinese people gathered to mark the first anniversary of Japan's surrender at a highly-charged political rally, openly organised by the Communist Party of Malaya and one to which (because of its theme) the British authorities could hardly object, much though they would have wished to.

Farrer Park was also the scene of many of the early PAP's campaigning rallies, even if no one rivalled the jolly theme of a 1958 Padang rally which attracted some 50,000 to witness the launch of the Anti-Spitting Campaign.

So, one final point. Just who was the Farrer who gave his name to this park? Well, he was the worthy if dullish R.G. Farrer who, during the 1930s, was in charge of the Singapore Improvement Trust home-building body and also a member of the Municipal Council. As the saying goes: Not a lot of people know that ...

When This was
Sin-Galore ...

Malay Street

Once the centre of Singapore's vice trade,
Malay Street was where 'you could be beaten up
and robbed for 50 cents, or knifed for a dollar.'

It's one of those neat little ironies which modern Singapore
can throw up. The new Bugis Junction complex boasts of
the region's first covered-over air-con shophouse streets within
its bulk. One such street was, in a previous life, Malay Street.
And Malay Street was the centre of Singapore's vice trade,
from the turn of this century up to 1930. Bugis Junction is one
of those family-fun joints. Hardly surprising then, that it has
chosen not to turn Malay Street into a historic mini-themepark,
evoking that for which it was previously so well-known.

For once, the sole door-by-door business of Malay Street
was the provision of sex-for-sale services. For tourists in search
of exotic Sin-Galore; for locals in search of a little light relief;
for any man with enough dollars in his pocket.

Steamers berthing at Keppel Harbour were greeted by
rickshaw-pullers or cabbies who would ask likely-looking male
arrivals: 'Malay Street, Boss?' Often, rickshaw men who spoke
no English would assume that Caucasian males must want
Malay Street and would grunt their way there, even if there
were protests from their passengers. In town, curious guests
staying at Raffles Hotel would gingerly step out on the short
stroll to this noted vice-den, responding perhaps to the hotel's
famous advice: 'When at The Raffles, why not see Singapore?'

Chinese hookers tended to keep away from Malay Street,
being usually based in Chinatown with its Blue Triangle
(formed by Keong Saik, Teck Lim and Jiak Chuan roads). It
was mainly Japanese 'Karayuki-san' girls, some 1,500 of whom

had fled depressed 1900s conditions in their homeland, plus Caucasian women who had frankly seen better days, plying their horizontal trade in Malay Street's cramped shophouses and catering for all-comers.

One observer of this red-light action was a British ex-rubber plantation manager turned journalist/intelligence agent, Bruce Lockhart. He noted vividly that the 1910s' Malay Street was 'where the white wrecks of European womanhood and young Japanese girls, silent, immobile and passionless, traded their bodies for the silver dollars of Malaya.'

Lockhart recalled a Madame Blanche and her 'collection of Hungarians, Poles and Russian Jewesses – a frail army of white women recruited by professional pimps from the poorest populations of central and eastern Europe, and drifting farther East as their charms declined, via Bucharest, Athens and Cairo, until they reached the "ultima Thrule" of their profession in Singapore.

'Sometimes a Malay princeling or Chinese "towkay" would make his way discreetly to this sordid temple (i.e. Malay Street) in order to satisfy an exotic and perhaps politically-perverted desire for the embraces of the forbidden white woman.'

Those Japanese women? Lockhart: 'Long rows of Japanese brothels with their lower windows shuttered with bamboo poles behind which sat the waiting "odalisques" (i.e. the girls), discreetly visible, magnificent in elaborate headdress and brightly-coloured kimonos, heavily painted and powdered, essentially doll-like and yet, not without a certain charm.'

Malay Street itself was decidedly without a certain charm. For as another observer observed: 'Here, you could be beaten up and robbed for 50 cents, or knifed for a dollar.' Plus, there was the menace of then-untreatable sexual diseases (though the Japanese women tried to impose some basic sexual hygiene, such as insisting their gentlemen visitors daub their ding-dongs in diluted potassium permanganate).

VD Epidemic!

The VD scare hit a peak in 1930, when an official commission reported the shock finding that nearly two-thirds of Singapore's male population then had some sort of sexual infection. Official alarm at this statistic provoked a 1930 clean-up clampdown, with Malay Street's brothels being forcibly closed and the freelance hookers lurking in its surrounding lanes and backstreets chased away. Women arriving from abroad who were suspected of seeking work on their backs, rather than on their feet or with their hands, were not allowed to even disembark.

Prostitution itself remained legal, so some of the evicted girls plied their trade along Dhoby Ghaut in what quickly became known as the 'rickshaw parade'.

The 'rickshaw parade ...'

The brothels themselves moved northwards to Lavender and Balestier, where they were thinly disguised as small hotels and lodging houses.

One major impact of the 1930 clampdown was noted by lawyer Roland Braddell in his *The Lights of Singapore* book: 'Sly prostitution and widespread venereal disease, ruined careers and broken health – a terrible price to pay for moral enthusiasms.' Braddell referred to another VD shock report, which came out in 1932, as proving that banning the brothels had been a mistake. For driving sex-for-sale underground (it

Lavender Street Stinks

Lavender Street got its delightful name as a rare official joke. For last century, it was a market gardening area which used 'night soil' (the polite Victorian term for manure, human and animal) as fertiliser. The stink this caused was so awful, the street was ironically called Lavender. A mellifluous name for a malodorous area!

A Dutch Wife for Will Rogers

The island's 1930s' reputation as Sin-Galore was not always justified. Noted American actor Will Rogers reported that the 'wickedest thing I found here was a Dutch wife in my bed.' A Dutch wife, of course, being not so much an Amsterdam adulteress as a stiff bolster pillow.

always being impossible to abolish) had achieved the opposite of controlling the spread of sexual diseases. 'Any old hand amongst the doctors will tell you why and what is to blame,' added Braddell.

Later in the 1930s, Malay Street took on a different character. Lockhart described it thus: 'The Europeans and Japanese had vanished. Like an army of ants, the Chinese had taken possession of the district, removing all vestiges of its former occupants.'

Such as those Japanese women, who had simply moved down the road a-piece and installed themselves within the fast-expanding Japanese community based around Middle Road. Here sprang up Japanese 'friendship houses' with their still kimono-clad hostesses overspilling out along Selegie Road. These continued to flourish – billed as gents' hairdressers, herbal parlours, traditional massage joints and the like (despite indignant letters to the press about the precise nature of their 'friendship').

Friendship houses ...

Sexual diseases also remained a problem. So much so that the Japanese community took its own measures by setting up a hospital called Do-jin to cater for Japanese hookers and their clients. After the Japanese Occupation, this was renamed as Middle Road hospital and it continued to serve in the front line against sexual diseases until 1988, when its functions were transferred to the DSC Clinic in Kelantan Lane, off Jalan Besar.

'Comfort Stations' in Syonan-To

When Yamashita's triumphant 25th Army took over the island in February 1942, most members of the Middle Road-based Japanese professional community revealed themselves as Fifth Columnists. Suddenly they were no longer courteous and charming – but 'brutality and arrogance was the order of the day', according to Senior Minister Lee Kuan Yew.

They had been waiting to link up with Singapore's new masters in controlling what was renamed Syonan-To (Light of the South). Among their willing volunteers were those Japanese prostitutes.

Soon Singapore had at least six 'comfort stations', the brothels set up by both the Tokyo government and the military command HQ all around Japan's imperial conquests in East Asia – and into which over 50,000 'comfort women' were forced. These women came mainly from Korea, the Philippines, China, Taiwan and Indonesia (including colonial Dutch women).

Singapore's comfort stations (for Japanese men only) were located as follows:

- *Pulau Bukom (now an oil refinery island);*

- *Sentosa (then called Blakang Mati, or 'Back of the Dead', because pirates once used it as a graveyard for their many victims);*

- *Nan Mei Su (Southern Beauties Resort) – a fenced-off row of shophouses at Cairnhill Circle where Cairnhill Hotel now stands;*

- *Tanjong Katong Road (shophouses between Wilkinson and Goodman roads);*

- *Chin Kang Huay Kuan clan association building at Bukit Pasoh; and*

- *The corner of Tras and Enggor streets (facing today's Amara Hotel on Tanjong Pagar Road). This was a two-storey residential unit 'staffed' by Taiwanese, Korean and Japanese women.*

Korean forced sex-labour women were sent to Sentosa, many of them having been told they were going to Syonan-To to work as waitresses at cafeterias for Japanese soldiers or nurses, or even merely to study.

Indonesian women were sent to Pulau Bukom, having been 'unloaded' at Keppel Harbour. They were usually young, aged between 14–20 – and many were dressed in white uniforms, as if to deceive them into thinking they really were being sent to Syonan-To to work as nurses.

According to a local Malay man also obliged to work on Pulau Bukom, these young Indonesians (most were virgins before arriving here) told him: 'It would be better if we died outside our homeland than if we went back with our bodies defiled.'

Singaporean 'Comfort' Women: Fact or Fiction?

Even 50 years afterwards, there is still local awkwardness about whether Singaporean women did or did not offer 'comfort' to the occupying Japanese army and its back-up civilians. For no known documented records exist of how Singapore's local prostitutes conducted themselves during those Japanese years of 1942–45.

But a letter-writer to *The Straits Times's Life!* section in September 1993 commented: 'There might have been imported sexual slaves but local prostitutes did not have any qualms about servicing Japanese soldier clients in the early Occupation days.

'Soon after the British surrender of Singapore, they (i.e. local prostitutes) resumed business promptly and the neighbourhood of Tanjong Pagar, which boasted call-girls of the select kind, was disturbed nightly by the boisterous entertainment of their Japanese officer clientele, who even took pains to familiarise the girls with martial songs.'

Yet a local consensus seems to have emerged that as so many Japanese prostitutes were working here before 1942, it was they who bore the brunt of the 'comforting'.

> **Four Hundred Brothels and 32 Million Condoms**
> It emerged in early 1993 that Tokyo's wartime military command in 1942 had made plans for over 400 comfort stations around its new Empire of the Sun – and was prepared to stock them with 32 million condoms!

Indeed, at a 1992 business seminar in Japan, Senior Minister Lee Kuan Yew (who never pulls his punches when discussing Japan's appalling wartime record) said that he believed it was already-experienced Japanese and foreign prostitutes who staffed Singapore's comfort houses, and who had thus 'saved the chastity of many Singaporean girls'. Now-old women from countries such as Korea, Taiwan and the Philippines have been coming forward since 1991 to demand apologies and compensation from Tokyo for forcing them into wartime prostitution.

Then in August 1993, a new Tokyo government finally committed Japan to an open public and official admission that its wartime Imperial Army had forced so many Asian women into prostitution – or, more accurately, into sex slavery.

A public and official admission ...

Even so, no compensation or apology claims on the comfort women issue has yet to emerge from Singapore. That's despite the way Dr Ong Chit Chung, a military historian, put it: 'There is no documented evidence of Singaporeans being comfort women, but there is always the possibility.'

Five-Sixty at the Blue Triangle

In the post-Occupation years, Singapore's sex trade located itself in small hotels and guest houses around the Selegie-Jalan Besar-Lavender-Balestier areas. These joints were even a little snobbish, often preferring Caucasian male customers to locals (who grumbled at how white men had pushed the prices up to $20 a crack).

The locals-preferring end of the flesh market rooted itself off Desker Road, while Chinese punters stuck to Chinatown's Blue Triangle – whose women were on offer at the standard charge of $5.60 (this quirky 'five-sixty' rate still raises a smile from old-timers).

The Desker Road price-per-quickie stayed at around $6 during the 1950s, but this back alley (which tourists were advised to avoid for fear of attack and robbery by thugs) won itself a shocking reputation for those easily shocked. Such as local journalist Sit Yin Fong, who in a 1954 newspaper column, under the vivid headline 'I Am Ashamed Of This', wrote: 'Desker Road is a picture of human tragedy ... In an ill-lit, stinking back lane, clusters of Chinese women stand at the open back doors of a long row of shophouses ... They are there for "inspection", as one might inspect cattle at a sale ... Vice is cheap here – the cheapest in the city. A woman can be had for the price of three beers ... there is no worse end ...' And so on.

It's all still there too, in much the same way, running along the whole length of the back alley between Desker and Rowell roads.

Early PAP Clampdown

A modern-era vice clampdown came in 1959, shortly after Singapore became a self-governing state. The early PAP, regarding sex-for-sale as colonial-era 'yellow culture' (along with skin-flick movie joints, the remaining opium dens, cockfight pits and such like), ordered police action to shut down the centrally-located little hotels, lodging houses and clip-joints.

But, just as in the 1930s, the clampdown hardly abolished prostitution. This time round, it just got pushed out of town, out of sight and into the suburbs. Above all, sex-for-sale was driven westwards to the private houses and bungalows along Geylang's narrow *lorongs*. The area from Lorongs 4–24, between Geylang and Guillemard roads, is now a zone which Singapore's vice business still calls home.

Wild Nights at Bugis Street

By the earliest 1960s, Bugis Street was well into its stride as a wild kind of place seemingly known as such around the world. Not alone for its Ah Quahs (beautiful but of uncertain sexual identity), also for the female-as-nature-intended women who would make their way to Bugis Street around midnight to parade themselves in front of tables where men were enjoying their beers.

One 1970s enthusiast wrote in *The Original Singapore Sling Book*: 'I used to sit there and think that Bugis Street must be one of the most beautiful streets in the world in its own way, because of its lights and the ever-changing crowds and because of its irresistible activity.

One of the most beautiful streets in the world ...

'It is civilised because of its merciful, uncritical tolerance. Nothing matters here, and the chief sins are not to smile and not to pay. All this is displeasing to authority, and many attempts have been made to do away with Bugis Street on one pretext or the other, but somehow it survives. Perhaps these attempts have succeeded by now ...'

Sure enough, in 1980, Bugis Street was shut down. And wiped off the map to make way for Bugis MRT station. Though the MRT's PR manager did concede in Cathay Pacific's in-flight mag *Discovery* (July 1993 edition) that: 'The construction of Bugis station could probably have been carried out without serious disruptions to Bugis Street.'

In 1991, Bugis Street was expensively brought back to life, in a faithful reconstruction of its original visuals, and on a site close to the original version. Initially there were hints that Ah

Quahs and their nocturnal female cousins would be 'encouraged' to return and add their own kind of atmosphere. Indeed, STPB adverts for the new Bugis appeared in Australian newspapers making **Les girls ...** this promise: 'And what of "les girls"? Let's just say we didn't go to all this effort just so you could have your fortune read ...'

Come opening night, however, there was hardly a hint of anything slightly naughty – and to this day, there still isn't. Bugis Street is merely a pretty open-air eating/drinking venue, and tourists on their Singapore-by-Night whizz-rounds must wonder what all the Bugis fuss was ever about. Meanwhile, the nearby base camp for Ah Quahs, Johore Road (Japanese trishaw-ride tourists would pay for photos of themselves posing alongside its impossibly-gorgeous creatures), has since also disappeared off the map. Following mysterious fires in 1991, every Johore Road shophouse was flattened and the site awaits a new role in life.

There are now fewer Ah Quahs here anyhow, as Singapore has ceased being the regional centre for sex-change operations. This is now very much Bangkok, where over 300 sex-change ops are conducted each year – with 'customers' coming from as far as Japan, the US and Europe. This operation is said to cost $9,200 to change a man into a woman and double that for the other way around.

Middle Road's 30,000 Victims

In March 1965, Mr Yong Nyuk Lin, the then Minister of Health, visited Middle Road Hospital and said that it was then treating over 30,000 VD victims. Mr Yong described prostitution as a 'social evil', but was pragmatic enough to add: 'A puritanical approach towards this age-old problem will not solve anything. If at all, such an unrealistic attitude will only make the social problem worse, to fester and spread underground.'

Also in 1965, a Middle Road medical officer observed that for every single VD case the hospital was treating, there 'must be at least five others' who had gone to private doctors and 'another five' who were trying traditional herbal remedies from Chinese *sinsehs* and Malay *bomohs*.

The same gloomy picture was painted a decade later by another Middle Road VD specialist, Dr V.S. Rajan. He said the 1974 VD figures were 18.2 per 100,000 population for syphilis and 149.2 for gonorrhoea. But the real local figures, he warned, were much higher.

Middle Road Hospital was then trying to encourage the use of condoms by prostitutes and their clients, with Dr Rajan noting that 75% of the VD casualties seeking medical treatment had received their infections from 'call-girls, dance hostesses, bar girls and social escorts'.

Fast-forward to 1994, and the sexual infection picture is much the same. Except for one terrifying newcomer: Aids. Singapore's first HIV-positive case was diagnosed (at Middle Road Hospital) in April 1983. Initially, this disease affected mainly homosexuals but by 1994, it had become primarily a heterosexual male problem.

Of the 854 reported HIV-positive cases in Singapore (by August 1998), a total of 176 had full-blown Aids while 282 had already died of Aids-related diseases. The vast majority (600) were men infected by prostitutes or casual sex partners (59 were wives infected by their errant husbands/boyfriends), while 126 were homosexual and 95 bisexual. The age group most affected was 20–39 years (579), followed by 40–49 (208). Some 18 people under the age of 20 were HIV-positive.

Last Words from Raffles

Prostitution has always has been in Singapore, ever since and even since Stamford Raffles set up his East India Company's 'emporium' in 1819. Before he finally left Singapore in 1823, Raffles wrote: 'The unfortunate prostitute should be treated with compassion, but every obstacle should be thrown in the way of her service being a source of profit to anyone but herself.'

The realistic Raffles knew that his bold new island enterprise would attract footloose men from all around Asia, and that **Footloose men ...** it would also require women to 'service' those men – and often to raise themselves out of poverty through what was then about the only female career opportunity.

Raffles's words signalled his contempt for pimps, those middlemen who creamed off their cuts from what women earned the hard way. A viewpoint shared by most such working women, both then and now ...

Informal Royal Palace

Istana Kampong Glam
Sultan Gate

Amid hi-tech towers and swirling traffic stands
a Malay royal palace that is a direct link to
modern Singapore's earliest history ...

This must be the world's friendliest, most informal royal palace complex. For royal indeed is the Istana Kampong Glam and its grounds between Sultan Gate and North Bridge Road. For a start, the old name for the palace and the various Malay aspects that radiate around its grounds is Kota Raja, or 'royal town' (there's even a little Kota Raja Kelab – social club – inside the complex). It's all a whole world apart from the modern towers of Beach Road and the swirling road traffic on its other side.

A whole world apart ...

Passing through the pastel yellow pillars of the open gateway, the 1840-built (and now decaying) Istana Kampong Glam holds pride of place. All open doors and windows, it overlooks an affable shambles of a compound with parked cars and little homes everywhere, with all sorts of everyday chores and activities going on.

Small children play happily, people pass here and there, everyone knows everyone's business. The compound looks and feels like a self-contained, spacious Malay kampong unit that has somehow escaped the relentless urbanisation of today's Singapore.

That's because the 80 or so people living either in the big house or the surrounding huts, are in some way related to the Sultan with whom Stamford Raffles did his 1819 business. Which means that, just as with the remains of the Temenggong's Telok Blangah village, Istana Kampong Glam is a direct link with modern Singapore's earliest history.

Succession Squabble

When Sultan Mahmud died in 1812 on Bintan island, there was an undignified squabble over the succession to the Riau-Johor Sultanate. Mahmud had left behind two sons by Bugis 'commoner' mothers: the Bugis supported his second son, Abdul Rahman; the Malays his first-born, Hussein. What swung it Rahman's way was Dutch support in 1818, thereby leaving Hussein with no domain over which to reign. Until the British arrived the next year.

Raffles sent for Hussein almost as soon as his troupe had struck camp by the Singapore river. Hussein approached gingerly, still so wary of the Dutch that he feared his summons was really a Dutch plot that would bring more harm his way.

So Hussein had put the word around Bintan that he was simply off on a fishing trip. Then he switched boats midway for a 'royal prahu' that deposited him on Singapore, where Raffles signed his treaty on 6 February with 'His Highness the Sultan Hussein Mohammed Shah, Sultan of Johor' (and separately with the Temenggong). Hussein was lured by the thought of regaining what he regarded as his stolen royal inheritance; Raffles achieved a legitimisation for his 'land grab' (as the Dutch saw it).

Raffles flattered Hussein and soothed his worries. Even if the reality was that the British were dealing with a man they despised, but found useful. For Hussein was an unlovely man, by all accounts. And certainly by the account of Munshi Abdullah, Raffles's Malay secretary: 'When he had become Sultan at Singapore, his body enlarged ... and his size became beyond all comparison. He was as broad as he was long, a shapeless mass. His head was small, and sunk into his shoulders from fat, just as if he had no neck ... he was potbellied in folds ... his voice husky, with an awful sound; and it was his custom to fall asleep whenever he sat down.

The Father of Malay Literature

Regarded by many as 'The Father of Modern Malay Literature', Munshi Abdullah was born in 1797 in Malacca, where he learned English from the town's colonial overlords. Munshi acted as interpreter and secretary for Stamford Raffles, and by 1822 he was operating a Singapore-based printing press which produced many Malay books. In 1840, he published his own memoirs called *Hikayat Abdullah*.

He died in Jeddah in 1854 while on a *haj*, or pilgrimage, to Mecca. He is noted in today's Singapore by Munshi Abdullah Avenue/Walk in Sembawang Hills' condo-land.

'I have never seen so unwieldy a man, he could not even carry his own body. And, to my apprehension, in such enormity there can be no pleasure or ease to the body, but nothing but trouble.'

Nothing but trouble was to follow. Hussein might have had his $5,000 Spanish dollars per year from Raffles's East India Company and his royal compound reaching from seafront to Rochor river, but with a sense of security settling upon his ample shoulders, he did too much that was unwise. Such as with the incident of his female sex slaves ...

Tortured lovelies fleeing the Sultan's harem was a final straw for the colony's stern second Resident, John Crawfurd (this Scotsman gave his name to the district bordering on today's Kampong Glam). Crawfurd was aware that the 1824 treaty with the Dutch meant there was now no need to appease the Sultan. So for starters, Crawfurd had a road built through the royal compound, cutting its access to the Rochor river and reducing it to its current (though still ample) 10,000 sq m.

Hussein's fortunes continued to decline; his physical condition likewise. In 1830, a European visitor described him thus: 'He appeared not even to possess the intelligence of an

Hussein's Sex Slaves

In 1824, 27 beautiful but tormented royal concubines escaped from Hussein's compound under cloak of darkness to seek the protection of British authority. The women described how they had been beaten with rattan canes, hung up, burned with pitch and punished by being made to go without food and without any clothing.

One of them disrobed to show the marks on her back, and British officials quickly agreed to 'resettle' the women – themselves taking first choice of the prettiest. Others went into Indian and Chinese homes, some to European ones, depending on who was offering food and shelter.

orang-utan … he appeared every moment to be in danger of an attack of apoplexy.'

A sexual scandal …

Hussein's wife, a more practical type, called in a Tamil merchant named Abdul Kadir to help sort out her family's increasingly hopeless financial mess. But this twosome's relationship provoked a sexual scandal (justified or not is unknown). A broken man, Hussein crept away from Singapore in 1834 for Malacca where he died the next year.

The Temenggong's Star Rises

He was succeeded as Sultan by his son Ali Iskandar Shah, who commissioned the handsome Istana Kampong Glam (its architect is thought to have been G.D. Coleman). But Sultan Ali's power and influence waned as Temenggong Ibrahim's rose across town at Telok Blangah. Ali's followers slipped away and his debts mounted to such a point that he had to pledge his annual government pension to a chettiar moneylender simply to service those debts.

So in 1855, under British supervision, he did a deal with his Temenggong. This meant Ali kept the title of Sultan and was promised a fixed annual pension. But also that the Temenggong (by rank, his subordinate) was now technically the ruler of Johor-Singapore. Technically, because the British were, of course, the ones really in charge.

Ali died in 1877, still heavily in debt. He was succeeded by his son Allum (or Along) who lived in the Istana for 14 years till his death in 1891. Allum was the man who in 1886 lost the official title of Sultan of Johor to Temenggong Abu Bakar.

When Allum died, his half-brother Mahmoud took over. In 1904, the British authorities ruled that although the original Sultan's descendants were allowed to use the Istana and its grounds, the ownership rights belonged to the then Colony of Singapore which would redistribute earnings from the estate back to the Sultan's descendants.

In disgust Mahmoud moved out of the Istana, though he hardly moved far. He stayed in the Gedong Kuning ('yellow mansion') still there today on Sultan Gate, just to the left of the Istana gateway.

The present-day supervisor of this historic site is the Public Works Department. The compound now houses some 20 families of whom, it is said, just three can claim to be direct descendants of that original overweight Hussein. Other distant relatives drifted into the compound during the Japanese Occupation (the Japanese respected the Istana's authority and spent time and money on its upkeep), and have stayed there ever since.

Today's Singapore government is still committed to paying the annual sum of money to the Sultan's descendants that was pledged by Sir Stamford Raffles. In 1991, this was capped at $250,000 which, of course, becomes thinner the wider it is spread.

Controversial Plans for the Istana

The current government concept for the Istana and its grounds (coming under the Kampong Glam conservation plan) is

Glam Wonder Oil

Glam is not short for glamour. The name comes from the gelam tree (also known as paper-bark tree) which once flourished in this area. Cajupute oil is extracted from the gelam's leaves, and is a crucial ingredient in the noted old Kampong Glam-made Boxing Ring Brand embrocation.

Recommended for all sorts of sporting aches and pains (the Harlem Globetrotters were said to use it) as well as for the tummies of women who've just given birth and 'wind on the skin' (whatever that is), Boxing Ring's little shophouse-based factory was forced out of Kampong Glam by the current conservation drive.

controversial. For the Istana's then headman, Tengku Abdul Aziz bin Tengku Hussein, had to be sharply told that redevelopment plans were not his to undertake as his family had not owned the actual land since 1904, and only the government could make major change-of-use decisions. So proposals were announced to restore the Istana and its compound into what would be regarded the jewel of a Kampong Glam conservation zone.

At first, this suited Tengku Aziz who suggested that modern apartments be built within the compound grounds for the Istana's dwellers. As he said: 'This is a great place to grow up and bring up kids. It is spacious and convenient as it is very near the city.'

Tengku Aziz died in November 1996. He was 53 years old and had finally lost his seven-year battle with diabetes and kidney failure. This sixth-generation direct descendant of the original Sultan Hussein died fittingly at his Kampong Glam royal palace. Tengku Aziz left behind a wife, four children and six grandchildren – but the line of succession to that Sultan of Singapore title remains unclear. As his son, 27-year-old

Meanwhile, in Jakarta …

Another direct descendant of the original Sultan Hussein is Tengku Haji Sari Indra, who has kept well out of all the Istana Kampong Glam's current uncertainties by settling in Jakarta with his family.

But he has with him a valuable souvenir of Singapore's Kota Raja: Sultan Hussein's original silver royal seal, plus 100-odd other heirlooms from his family's past. He's big on antiques and says he's keeping the Kampong Glam heirlooms because he doesn't want them 'falling into the hands of people who do not appreciate them'.

Tengku Damaishah, said: 'What we have is only the name of being descendants of Sultan Hussein, and a rich family history. Other than that, we are Singaporeans. We go through National Service like everyone, and work to make a living. Actually, some of us live in HDB flats.'

An idea to convert the Istana building itself into a Malay Heritage Centre is not so popular. The compound's families feel that kind of thing should be based at Geylang's Malay Village (which is certainly still searching for a viable role). One resident, Tengku Ishak, broke into mellifluous, if fluffy, Malay to state his case. In translation: 'As long as the sun and the moon exist, the palace cannot be taken away from us to be converted into a museum.'

The Kampong Glam conservation has already seen the pedestrianisation of half of Bussorah Street. This may now look lovely but is largely lifeless, as those who lived and/or worked here in the two-storey state-owned shophouses flanking the street were required to leave before their 'makeovers'. As *Straits Times Life!* journalist Ida Bachtiar wrote in April 1993: 'It remains to be seen whether the place will retain its historical integrity or become another commercial showcase of Surprising Singapore.'

Memories of a more glorious past – Istana Kampong Glam today.

One 1992 letter-writer to *The Straits Times* had not been so restrained. Noting that already-atmospheric Bussorah Street did not owe its charm to 'facades and motifs' nor did it need 'any form of beautification', the writer sighed: 'Our culture is fast disappearing as we continue to yearn for everything to look all clean and dressed up.' Then, a final plea: '... prevent Singapore from being turned gradually into a giant Hollywood studio.'

Even if an air of uncertainty hangs over the place, at least the old Kota Raja – bounded by Victoria Street, Beach Road, Rochor Road and Jalan Sultan – is still there to be savoured.

So there's still time to appreciate this section of Singapore for what it is: a timeless world all of and on its own. The tombstone makers on Pahang Street; the Malay barbers of North Bridge Road; the old Malay graveyard off Victoria Street; the *nasi padang* joints of Kandahar/Bussorah streets; the batik, basketware and ethnic shops of Arab Street; Islamic Restaurant (dating from 1921, it's probably Singapore's oldest restaurant); 'The Leaning Tower of Singapore' – Hajah Fatimah

A timeless world ...

The Final Curtain?

The uncertainty hovering over Istana Kampong Glam was finally resolved in April 1999, when the government ruled that the palace would indeed become a Malay Heritage Centre. And that all the people currently living in the Kota Raja compound would have to move out. Sweetening the pill was a promise to boost the allowances granted to all 80 descendants of the original Sultan – they will now share $350,000 per annum for 30 years.

One such, Tengku Damaishah, remained churlish, even if his personal 'pay rise' would be a leap from his current $23 per month to $51,000 (in lump sum payment form). He protested: 'The Istana is our birthright. How can we give it up just like that and sign away our property?'

Whatever, the new plan will see the government restore and conserve the historic Istana building (along with its neighbouring Bendahara House) before handing it over to a new body which will run the Malay Heritage Centre. Plus, a grant of up to $2 million to help establish a Heritage Centre Endowment Fund. In response to which, Tengku Damaishah had more dissenting words: 'It will be another dead Malay Village.' Only time will tell …

Mosque near Jalan Sultan; Istana Kampong Glam itself; Sultan Mosque (its site decreed by Hussein and agreed to by Raffles; the distinguished current building opened in 1928), with its calls to prayer and a little row of Muslim eating-houses right opposite.

Singapore's Airports

People's Association Headquarters Building
Old Kallang Airport Terminal, Stadium Link

Decades before Changi International, Kallang
was already dubbed 'the finest airport
in the British empire' …

As they speed along Nicoll Highway by the People's Association HQ building or surge into the National Stadium, people may not realise they're close to the centrepiece of what was in its time dubbed 'the finest airport in the British Empire'. There again, that time was more than 60 years ago …

For it was in 1930 that Sir Cecil Clementi arrived here from Hong Kong to take up his duties as Governor. One of his earliest priorities sprang from his realising that the world stood poised on the brink of a major transportation shift. That is, the dominance of sea travel was about to be usurped by airplanes.

Sir Cecil saw that Singapore needed a proper civilian airport to deal decisively with the opportunities offered by Singapore's

In a previous life, the PA HQ building was once the heart of Singapore's air links.

strategic location on the world map. No more could seaplanes be asked to splash down on gooey Balestier Plain; the old race course at what is now Farrer Park was hardly up to it; and Seletar airport had been opened in 1927 primarily for the Royal Air Force – even if it did provide a landing strip for early dashing aviators such as Amy Johnson and, on one notable occasion in November 1932, for then mega movie stars Douglas Fairbanks and wife Mary Pickford.

Sir Cecil decreed that there must be a new airport and got into a plane himself, flying low over the island several times to determine exactly where. He decided on the Kallang river basin, despite the huge cost (some $8 million, eventually) of the land reclamation project that would first be required.

In August 1931, he explained to the Legislative Council: 'Looking into the future, I expect to see Singapore become one of the largest and most important airports of the world. It is on the direct route to Australia and is bound to develop as a nodal point for air services in the course of time. It is therefore essential that we should have here, close to the heart of the town, an aerodrome which is equally suitable for land planes and for sea planes – and the best site, beyond all question, is the Kallang Basin.'

A Swamp is Transformed

The first map of the proposed Kallang airport was drawn up in 1932 and, given that the river lapped up to today's Mountbatten Road (then Grove Road), there was much basic work to be done before the airport itself could even be started. The area to be reclaimed covered some 339 acres, much of which was a pestilential tidal swamp. Over 200,000 tons of earth and rock were brought here each month along a temporary rail track from the Bedok area, where the ground was thus scooped out for today's Bedok Reservoir. By 1936, the Kallang river basin had been drained and smothered; work could then begin on the easier bit – the airport itself.

The airport was officially opened on 12 June 1937 with a jolly airshow, and the praise for its facilities and the 'ultramodern' look of its terminal building (yes, today's PA Building) was both lavish and unanimous. *The Straits Times's* excited headlines proclaimed: 'City has fine gateway to world's air lines. Giant sky ships bring Malaya close to Europe and America. Singapore has a new front door. For size and appearance, its only rival in Asia is said to be the airport at New Delhi.'

The finest airport in the British Empire ...

While in the words of a publication entitled *Wonders of World Aviation*: 'The city of Singapore can claim, for the present, to have the finest airport in the British Empire.'

Kallang Airport had a circular grassed-over landing area with its apron and taxiways in concrete, plus a concrete slipway for seaplanes on the basin side. That terminal building was regarded as an excellent example of the 'modern movement' – with its crisp, clean lines suggesting the look of an ocean liner or a seaplane. It was designed by the Public Works Department which had just finished the classical Supreme Court building on the Padang, and that is praise indeed for PWD's versatility.

Just 16 days after its official opening, Kallang was the base for the first internal Malayan air links when Wearne's Air Services unveiled its de Havilland DH-89 Dragon Rapide twin-engined eight-seater named 'Governor Raffles', with its scheduled flights to Kuala Lumpur ($30 one-way) and Penang ($50). But the most exciting sights at Kallang were the splashdown water landings of the luxurious (and pricey – air travel was not yet for the masses) British Imperial Airways Empire and Pan-Am Clipper flying boats.

In the light of today's stern no-smoking airline policies, the gracious language of the Imperial Airways publicity brochure sounds like another era in aviation: 'If you have succumbed to the lure of King Nicotine, it is no longer necessary to deprive yourself of the solace of your favourite "weed". A well-appointed smoking salon is provided.'

Kallang postponed its civilian air activities in 1941 as war engulfed the region. The subsequent Japanese Occupation left one lasting contribution to the airport through its use of forced labour to build a concrete runway over its grassy circle. This new runway was almost 1,700 metres long and 50 metres wide and would split today's National Stadium from the Kallang Theatre and the Singapore Indoor Stadium.

The First SIA Girl Takes Off

Kallang had returned to normal civil aviation by 1947. On 1 May of that year, the newly-formed Malayan Airways – predecessor of today's SIA – launched its first flights (to Kuala Lumpur, Ipoh and Penang) with a twin-engined Airspeed Consul. On board was who could be described as the first 'Singapore Girl' air stewardess, a Miss Rosemary Tay.

As the seaplane faded into aviation history, Kallang's days became numbered and Paya Lebar International Airport started to take shape from 1951 onwards (requiring the cutting-down of some 20,000 rubber and coconut trees for its 2,400 m runway). The urgency of the (expensive) switch-over became clear when the British 'wonder' Comet jets started arriving in 1951 (they did the London-Singapore trip in 20 hours' flying time) and found Kallang's runway dangerously short and its sea mist troublesome.

This urgency reached frenzy point when, on 13 March 1954, what is still Singapore's worst aviation disaster took place. A Qantas BOAC Constellation jet crashed as it tried to land, killing all 31 passengers and two crew members when it burst into flames. A dramatic photo of rescuers scrambling around this doomed airplane won Sam Kai Faye the 1955 World Free Press Photo competition.

The low approach over the often-misty waterfront was a contributing factor to this disaster and just over a year later, on 20 August 1955, the larger (safely inland) Paya Lebar airport was opened.

The Last Airspeed Consuls

There are just six British-made Airspeed Consuls left today, and one now graces the entrance of the new SIA Training Centre on Upper Changi Road. Made mainly from strong, pliable spruce plywood and capable of carrying just seven people (including two crew), the vintage plane – in a badly run-down condition – was bought in 1987 by Singapore Airlines as part of its 40th anniversary celebrations. The seller was the UK's Royal Air Force Museum, and some aviation buffs in Britain were unhappy. They felt its rarity and historical value meant it should have been restored and not sold to an 'outside party'.

For its part, SIA lovingly restored the plane to such a state that it could actually fly again, though this has not happened yet as the plane is purely for display. SIA paid some 2,000 British pounds (then about S$6,000) for its Airspeed Consul; enthusiasts would now pay up to $1 million for it. But SIA has no plans to sell its valuable 'toy'.

Kallang's terminal building was a popular place right up to its enforced retirement. Singaporeans would flock to its restaurant for fresh oysters from Australia and strawberries and cream from Tasmania. Then, in its final days, Kallang had a moment of extremely high political drama.

Zhou Enlai Cheats Death

On 17 April 1955, the Asia-Africa Conference was due to start in Bandung, West Java. This was the first international political conference involving the nonaligned states of Asia and Africa, and Indonesia's President Sukarno had invited delegates from 29 nations (from Singapore, trade unionist S. Woodhull had observer status, representing the PAP) to Bandung's Gedung Merdeka meeting hall.

The big cheeses at this eight-day conference were India, with its Prime Minister Pandit Nehru, and China, with its PM Zhou Enlai. But Zhou, Chairman Mao's designated successor until his death from cancer in 1976, nearly didn't make it.

The Constellation plane carrying Zhou and his party from Beijing was due to land at Kallang on its way to Java. Then news came through that it had been blown up over the sea just south of Hong Kong. A bomb had been placed in one of its fuel tanks (by a Hong Kong ground crew member who quickly skipped off to Taiwan and was handsomely rewarded by Chiang Kai-shek's Nationalist government).

Some 30 Chinese delegation members died in the explosion, and international news reporters rushed to Kallang airport in the expectation that the death list included Zhou Enlai. For such an assassination could have led to all-out war between China and Taiwan.

At Kallang, it was learned that Zhou had switched flights at the last minute, alerted by a tip-off from the Hong Kong communist intelligence network. A shaken but alive Zhou eventually arrived at Kallang on board a cumbersome Dakota plane around which

Shaken but alive ...

a strong security cordon was thrown, so strong it caused a minor diplomatic flap before completing its flight to Indonesia.

This was a fittingly dramatic curtain call for Kallang airport before it was replaced by Paya Lebar – which, in its turn, served its civil aviation role until Changi International Airport was opened on 12 May 1981. It now serves as a base for Singapore's Air Force (though mysteriously, it still doesn't appear in the official *Singapore Street Directory*).

Merdeka Debacle at Kallang

For want of another role in life, the old Kallang airport became a public park and on 18 March 1956, it hosted another dramatic moment in modern Singapore's history.

Yeah Yeah Yeah!

Causing most unseemly panic at the Paya Lebar airport in 1964 were the Fab Four, the moptopped Beatles then causing early-teen hysteria all around the world, and here on their way to Australia. Frenzy was the word, as police tried to hold back some 3,000 excited Singapore youngsters in the moist grip of Beatlemania, with steel barricades being stormed and access roads blocked off.

It was during this brief visit that the late John Lennon gave Raffles Hotel his own spin by calling it 'The Rattles'. The Rolling Stones also provoked much excitement at Paya Lebar the next year (they were here to play at the old Badminton Stadium on Guillemard Road). But it was only much later that Mick Jagger left his personal mark on Singapore.

Visiting here with his gorgeous wife Jerry Hall in 1979, the couple decided to chill out at the then Black Velvet disco (in what's now ANA Hotel off Tanglin Road). Only the doorman didn't recognise the couple and anyhow he thought Jagger was 'not dressed appropriately'. So he wouldn't let them in, no way. Local and world media had a whole heap of fun with that story ...

Then it was the scene of a 25,000-strong All-Party Merdeka ('Freedom') Rally. This was intended to mount a display of political and racial unity and a desire for full independence to cap 'Merdeka Week'. The then Chief Minister David Marshall had what he tagged his 'M-bomb' – eight Merdeka referendum books with 167,259 signatures calling for self-rule from Britain (with 128 against). The rally was also aimed to impress a visiting six-man fact-finding delegation of British MPs that the populist drive for independence was for real.

David Marshall's 'M-bomb' ...

After these MPs had witnessed it, the rally soon became a shambles. Groups of Chinese Middle School students did 'Red

Indian dances', which had become associated with communist supporters. An organised group of radicals shouted contrary slogans and then charged the police near the abandoned airport terminal. Other students hoisted a banner with Picasso's Peace Dove on it – again, recognised as a symbol of communist sympathies.

The amplifying sound equipment packed up, and while David Marshall was speaking on it, a crowd of people charged onto the temporary stage which had been erected on the old runway (through which Nicoll Highway was then being built). The platform collapsed, leaving over 50 people (including 20 policemen) injured – and later that night in town, there were more flare-ups.

All of which, as a 1956 government report suggested, was 'not the outcome which was expected nor the scene which was to have been presented to the visiting MPs.' What's more, David Marshall's credibility was thus weakened when he attended the first Merdeka talks in London, just four days later. He failed to get what he wanted from the British government and upon his return to Singapore, he stepped down as Chief Minister and head of the then-ruling Labour Front coalition (he was replaced by Lim Yew Hock). It was not till 1959 that Singapore got the go-ahead from London for full internal self-government.

A Prime Minister's Memories

In May 1994, Prime Minister Goh Chok Tong visited the splendidly-restored (at a cost of $4.16 million) People's Association building and gave this reaction: 'I was a little amazed at the small size of the arrival and departure hall … Compared to Changi, it's a miniature. It shows how fast Singapore has grown.' Mr Goh also revealed that, as a 14-year-old, he had been taken by his uncle to attend that 1956 Merdeka Rally at Kallang.

In August 1959, the old Kallang airport grounds, then overgrown with lallang grass and weeds, were chosen to kick off a 'Lungs For The People' campaign by the newly-independent Singapore as an early part of its drive to create a green 'garden city'. It was soon turned into a proper park with a playground, and the pleasing seafront promenade off Nicoll Highway was built with volunteer public help.

Then in 1974, the National Stadium was opened on what was the old airport's landing zone. What with the tennis and squash centre in this area, plus the People's Association (PA), Kallang Theatre and Singapore Indoor Stadium, Kallang's old airport grounds are today firmly established as the national sports and recreational centre.

The PA had been set up in 1960 as a 'community development agency' and it was happy to take over the old terminal building. Former Qantas hangars and other airport offices are still there today, shared by the PWD (the original

Concorde Capers

One too-brief visitor to the Paya Lebar airport was the sexy supersonic Anglo-French plane, Concorde. It first touched down here in 1972 for a guest appearance. The plane so impressed Singapore Airlines that by 1977 it had started a joint service from Paya Lebar with British Airways (one side of the Concorde in SIA livery, the other BA-style) on the Singapore-London route, taking a mere nine-and-a-half hours.

Early Malaysian objections to its loud sonic booms suspended the service temporarily, but then by 1980, it simply wasn't paying its way and had to cease. These days, this SIA Concorde can be spotted only on the back of local $20 bank notes, though oddly it shows the Concorde hovering over Changi Airport. Odd, because Changi didn't open for business till May 1981, a good six months after the Concorde service was finally terminated ...

builders) and by various other wholesome arms of the PA. Now around this landmark building in Singapore's aviation history, there is a running track, a croquet pitch, netball courts and other 'character-building' facilities.

No one expects the PA Building to offer oysters or strawberries and cream, but an old museum-piece seaplane on permanent show outside it might be a nice touch. Or even a little plaque to mark Sir Cecil Clementi's far-sighted decision in 1931, a decision that put Singapore so decisively on the world's aviation map. So much so that these days its superb Changi International Airport (with its Terminal 3 already planned) is a regular winner of World's Number One awards …

The End of the Worlds

The Entertainment Parks of Singapore
*Gay World, Geylang Road; Great World, Kim Seng Road;
New World, Jalan Besar*

Striptease, cabaret girls and boxing matches
were just some of the many attractions during
the heyday of the entertainment parks ...

The great Singaporean entertainment park was not invented by Runme Shaw. New World had already been put in place by the Ong brothers along Kitchener Road (between Serangoon Road and Jalan Besar) when Shaw arrived here from Shanghai in 1924. But he moved quickly to grab a 50% interest in New World, jazzing it up and introducing some Shanghai-style attractions. Soon business was booming, more so than at the rival Great World on Kim Seng Road (set up in the early 1930s).

In 1934, Roland Braddell wrote: 'At New World there are all sorts of entertaining sideshows. Best of all are the Malay opera and the Chinese theatrical performances which so fascinated Charlie Chaplin when he was here. We have another amusement park called the Great World, off River Valley Road, and it too is well worth a visit, but it is not so boisterously alive as is the New World, since it caters to a much smugger class.'

Shaw's New World charged 10¢ admission and played host to a wide range of hawkers alongside the Teochew/Hokkien *wayang* and Malay opera halls. These each also charged 10¢ but people prepared to watch them from the sides could see them for free. Nearby was an open-air stage for dancing, *joget-*style. New World also hosted boxing matches, featuring weekly tournaments with fighters from Australia, Thailand and the Philippines, as well as local pugilists. There was an unfortunate outcome at a New World bout in September 1934 when 21-

year-old Joe Thunderface from Pasadena, California died during his fight with local boy Frankie Weber.

New World had a Ghost Train, Dodg'ems and other fairground diversions. No wonder it advertised itself as the 'pioneer amusement park in Malaya', using slogans like: 'All the features associated with the business of fun-getting/Rich in colour and gay with music.' Plus: 'We lead, others follow.'

'We lead, others follow' ...

This was a dig at Singapore's third entertainment park, Happy World, which Lee Geok Eng set up in 1936 between Mountbatten and Geylang roads. Happy World retorted with its own jolly slogan: 'It's exciting, colourful, colossal! Fun's a-poppin' all over the place!'

The World of Tiger Lilies

The real War of the Worlds involved their lovely cabaret girls. Bruce Lockhart, a British army intelligence officer-cum-journalist, described thus his 1936 visit to New World: 'I went into the dancing-hall. There was an excellent orchestra hired, I think, from some liner. It was playing "Auf Wiedersehen" when I came in, and a crowd of dancers, mostly young Chinese – the men in white European clothes with black patent-leather dancing shoes, the girls in their semi-European dresses slit at the side – filled the dancing floor.

'When the dance was over, I noticed a number of girls who left their partner as soon as the music stopped and went to join other girls in a sort of pen. They were the professional Chinese dancers who can be hired for a few cents a dance.' Lockhart was describing the cabaret girls, or taxi-girls – that is, they were 'for hire'. Men would buy a book of four 25¢ dance tickets and hand over

Dirty Dancing, *Ang-mo*-style

Dancing was a different matter among the stiffer sections of the 1930s' colonial community. Full evening dress including coat-tails (though sometimes, white jackets were permitted) were required at Raffles Hotel and such like snob venues. If an 'improperly' dressed man took to The Raffles's dance floor, the orchestra would stop playing until he had left again. As Bruce Lockhart noted, unlike the Worlds' vivacity: 'Raffles appeared to me more decorous and more middle-class than any Bournemouth hotel on a Sunday.'

The blame for all this stiff stuff was placed on those English wives and female relatives who flocked out to 1920/30s' Singapore and tried to impose some 'social order' on the easy-going ways of their menfolk. Ian Morrison noted neatly in his 1942 *Malayan Postscript*: 'The white woman has inevitably tried to recreate England, and usually Surbiton (note: a drearily 'respectable' London suburb), in the tropics.' Little wonder the men were always trying to sneak off to a World of their own!

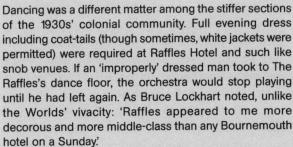

a ticket to their chosen partner. But for dancing only, as Lockhart found out from one Chinese cabaret girl who gloried in the name of Tiger Lily.

'Breaches of discipline are severely punished. They are paid about eight cents a dance. Each dance is registered on a card, and at the end of the week, the cards are vigilantly scrutinised. Girls who are in great request may be promoted. Others have their wages reduced. The decorum was unimpeachable. To me this model seemliness was even more extraordinary than the almost complete waiving of the colour bar in a British colony.'

These cabaret dances soon proved the biggest attraction in the Worlds, with Great having a huge and swanky dance floor that could take up to 500 couples (a dance floor it acquired from the demolished Hotel de l'Europe). The cabaret girls – 'the most beautiful dance hostesses' – were usually local/Hong

Kong Chinese or Eurasian, with a sprinkling of Indians, Malays, Thais, Indo-Chinese and Filipinas.

Cabaret girls were not call-girls; they were indeed often straight-laced and no naughty business was expected or allowed from their male partners. At New World, the girls even had their own security force – burly bouncers who dealt with problems arising from boozed-up men who expected a bit more than just a twirl around the dance floor.

The girls had bigger problems meeting the bills for the clothes and hairdos that would keep their dance-cards marked. For basic salary was $25 a month, together with 40 percent of ticket takings. This went up for the 'superstars' of the cabaret floor, the girls who were not paid any basic fee but who could keep all their ticket takings.

A Bosomy Human Cannonball

One such was Anita Gonzales, a Filipina and a favourite of the Sultan of Johor who would pay her $100 to hear her sing just for him. Her voice was said by others within earshot to be suspiciously 'half man and half woman'.

Other World-class diversions included shows by visiting entertainers, such as the all-singing, all-dancing De Souza Sisters who introduced themselves thus:

> 'Singapore, hulloa, hulloa!
> In silk and satin and boa
> We are the girlies from Goa!'

Or Miss Olive Kennedy-Walsh, BA (Arts), H Dip Ed, the surely over-qualified English 'human cannonball' with an inconveniently large bosom (her breasts got stuck in the Great World cannon rim and had to be kneaded inside by helpful cabaret girls).

Cabarets at the Worlds started coming to life around 7 pm, closing at midnight during the week and at 1 am on Saturdays. On weekends, there were also 4 pm tea dances for which one dollar would buy three dances; two dollars, six. Chinese businessmen liked 'give-face' displays of their wealth by hiring a half-dozen or so girls for the one dance, which often took the form of a haphazard conga. One 'towkay' paid dearly for this ostentation by suffering a fatal heart attack while being playfully pushed around the dance floor by five girls.

The food was also out of this World, with Great's Chinese restaurants much in demand for wedding, birthday and Lunar New Year dinners. After which, guests could easily slip over to the cabaret floor – and those girls. New too bragged about its 'superb' Chinese restaurant.

Hard Times at the Worlds

The Japanese Occupation meant inevitable restrictions. The cabarets were closed (New's air-con dance hall had been destroyed anyhow by a Japanese direct-hit bomb); the parks were more noted for their stalls selling black-market 'goodies' at hugely-inflated prices (chocolates, cigarettes, etc, mainly from Red Cross PoW parcels 'rediverted' by Japanese officers).

After 1945, there was time to be made up: the entertainment parks roared back into life. The cafes put on singers, bringing Allied soldiers into their Worlds in droves. Then, with the departure of those troops, new tricks were needed. Such as? Striptease!

Striptease arrives ...

Striptease arrived in 1949 courtesy of Madame Tai Fong, a former singer and dancer. She started up the Fong Fong Revue in New World, introducing new dances and comedy routines, with exciting new costumes for her girls. And the first known striptease public entertainment in Singapore.

Madame Tai's revues were soon pulling in spectacle-starved spectators, who responded most joyfully to the frisky Fong Fong 'Butterfly Dance' routines. Until, that is, spoilsport colonial police moved in too to insist that two Fongs did not make a right and that all this monkey business must cease.

Striptease was thus stopped in its tracks but in time, it re-emerged elsewhere. During the early 1960s, Minh-Kim (the self-styled Princess of Hanoi) created a splash with her revealing shows at Malaysia Hotel, predecessor of today's Boulevard Hotel. She even had helpful career advice for young women thinking of following her trade.

'The projection of erotic appeal is something which is natural to all women but extensive training, rehearsals and a thorough study of the male mind are necessary if a young girl wishes to take up the sensual art of striptease.' She added, reassuringly, that an 'enormous chest' was not always necessary.

Another 1960s star of the striptease art came from New York. This was Miss Marquise Diamond, who said of her work: 'Stripteasing comes naturally to me. So much so that I love to expose my body (note: which was 35-23-35) to the audience.'

When the Queen of Strip Ruled the Worlds ...

Above all, and showing all, there was Rose Chan. China-born but Singapore-raised, she was the local 'Queen of Strip' who took her public disclosure skills around the Worlds and the world, though she took up her vocation only at 27 (during the late 1950s).

There was nothing coy or shy about Rose Chan. She stripped completely, she teased totally and then wandered, clad merely in high-heels and perfume, through her enraptured audiences. She had it, she flaunted it; never more so than with her famous python act. This involved an enormous (if doped) snake, with which Rose cavorted by coiling it provocatively round her barely-clad body. No wonder it was said that as she took her show around the towns of Singapore and Malaya, 'husbands disappeared'.

Her memory lingers. In 1994, author Catherine Lim wrote of her: 'Chan would have laughed in scorn at the furore that greeted the famous Sharon Stone act in the film *Basic Instinct*. In the sheer uninhibitedness of her instinct to please and tease, she certainly out-Stoned Stone, just as in her indefatigable taking of one husband after the other, she out-Taylored Elizabeth Taylor.'

Alas, a poor Rose Chan died miserably of cancer in 1989 in Penang. She was 62. Her mourners were many.

Coming of the End

Come the 1960s, more sophisticated times arrived and the Worlds declined rapidly in the face of rival entertainment attractions, particularly that of television (which took off here in 1963). In brief, they became Olde Worlds, despite a short boom in trade fairs.

Great World was closed down in 1964. Its five football fields-sized site is now covered by the huge and handsome Great World condo-office-shopping complex. New World closed in the mid-1980s, and its cleared site was only finally under redevelopment by mid-1994. Meanwhile, Happy World (which, in a reversal of the global trend, renamed itself Gay World along the way) still has much within its Geylang walls to recall erstwhile jollities.

Seven Storeys

Still hanging on, if now in splendid isolation on its cleared Rochor Road site, is the hotel with the boastful name 7th Storey Hotel (so near the 73-storey Westin Stamford!). But in the 1950s, the 7th Storey had its hotspot Harlequin nightclub on the sixth level.

As the advert boasted: 'It overlooks the harbour, and here one can dine and dance in cool air-conditioned comfort. There is an excellent choice of Chinese and European menus to be had, plus a lively dance band.' Now the 7th Storey offers more modest *makan* – the coffeeshop at street level, which comes without a dance band in residence. But this Hainanese kitchen does dish up a delicious old-style charcoal-boiled steamboat!

Such as its former indoor sports hall, once billed as the 'Greatest Covered Stadium in Southeast Asia'. Inside here were staged many memorable wrestling matches, as *Under One Roof* actor/comedian Moses Lim recalled: 'My heroes had names like Tiger Ahmad and King Kong. You scream, you shout while they were jumping on each other and smashing chairs over their opponents' heads.'

But the Gay future is now unclear, with the stalls and halls once so vibrant now used by motor-repair shops and furniture

An uncertain future ...

showrooms. At least it can still boast of Singapore's smallest movie house, called New Happy Cinema and specialising now in Indian films. What's more, just opposite on Geylang Road, a new boutique hotel opened in 1997 under the name Gay World Hotel – which could well mislead some visiting tourists! And the complex still has its handsome if decayed entrance gates, through which once flocked more innocent and more happily-entertained Singaporeans.

This story ceases with the end of the Worlds. In their time, they truly were New, Great and – er, um – Gay ...

Singapore Goes Berserk

The 1964 Geylang race riots
Kallang gasworks, junction of Lavender Street and Kallang Road

When six days of racial insanity nearly tore
the island apart ...

Singapore today is justly proud of and carefully sensitive to its racial and religious harmony, of how its people from such different cultures can live together as neighbours in mutual understanding and tolerance. It's a state of civic harmony not easily achieved, as the world's headlines continue to testify. Yet six days of racial insanity in 1964 meant that modern Singapore's multiracial society was nearly torn apart before it had the chance to even take root.

Savage race riots broke out on 21 July 1964, the day of the Prophet's birthday. That afternoon, some 25,000 Malay Muslims had gathered on the Padang for the occasion, after which they set off in an enormous procession to snake their way to Geylang. Shortly after 5 pm, there was a sudden outbreak of violence. Small-scale, but it quickly led to insanity stalking the streets of Singapore, where people of both dominant races were quickly going berserk and running amok. It was if the local racial mix had been a dry powder keg, awaiting only a single carelessly-lighted match.

The rioting and intercommunal violence between Chinese and Malays was furthermore exploited by various criminal and gangster elements, plus people bearing grudges they found they suddenly had a chance to exploit. Thus within two hours of the original Kallang gasworks flare-up, violence had spread to the town centre. By the end of that night, outbreaks were happening on virtually an islandwide basis.

The race riots finally subsided after six angry days – with a casualty list of 23 dead and 454 injured. For two weeks, police

The Maria Hertogh Riots

In December 1950, 18 people were killed and over 180 injured in the street violence which followed a Singapore High Court ruling that young Maria Bertha Hertogh should be returned to her mother (Adelaine, an ethnic Malay with Dutch citizenship) and father in the Netherlands.

Because her parents were imprisoned during the Japanese occupation of Indonesia, Maria had been brought up and effectively adopted (as a Muslim with the name Nadra) by the family nurse Aminah. Post-war, the parents launched a search for their daughter, eventually tracking her down in Terengganu. Just before the Singapore court case came up, Maria was deliberately married off (as a 13-year-old) to a 21-year-old Malay schoolteacher, Mansoor Adabi. When the Singapore court ruled this marriage was invalid (under then-relevant Dutch law) and that Maria should be returned to her parents, this was interpreted as an insensitive colonial decision offensive to Islam – and the mainly-Malay rioting broke out.

Maria was last heard of in 1976 when charged with the attempted murder of the Dutch soldier with whom she had eloped. She was acquitted, and afterwards moved away from her family. Her vivid story was the subject of an excellent SBC 1993 docu-drama, entitled 'My Name Is Nadra, Not Bertha'. The SBC producers could not track Maria down to cooperate in the programme's making.

enforced a curfew (ending on 2 August) which at first ran each day from 9 pm–6 am, causing the streets to empty of people and traffic, a rash of event cancellations, *Panic in the markets ...* panic in the markets and stores and the prices of everyday items soaring to three times their normal cost.

The community damage caused by all this took longer than a fortnight to heal. There was indeed a second, if more localised, outbreak of racial violence in Geylang for a week in

September 1964 which left 12 dead and 109 injured. They added up to Singapore's worst racial flare-ups since the Maria Hertogh riots in 1950. Today, thankfully, it's all so unimaginable ...

The Spark That Set off the Madness

The exact flare-up point on 21 July was close to the now demolished Kallang gasworks, by the junction of Lavender Street and Kallang Road. What ignited that gasworks spark remains an issue of some dispute. Singapore Prime Minister Lee Kuan Yew went on the radio at 10.45 that night to blame Malays straggling at the end of the procession for attacking a Chinese policeman after he had ordered them to keep up with the main body of people. 'Instead of being obeyed,' said Mr Lee, 'he was set upon by them. Thereafter, a series of disturbances occurred as more groups became unruly and attacked passers-by and spectators.'

Tun Abdul Razak – acting Malaysian (Singapore then being part of the new Federation) Prime Minister while Tunku Abdul Rahman was away in the US – took a different view of how it had started. He claimed that a hostile individual among the Chinese onlookers along the side of the road had thrown a glass bottle at the procession.

An official inquiry was supposed to have been held in April 1965 by Mr Justice Chua but no more was heard of this, with other more pressing and immediate events rapidly overtaking its purpose. It was probably a wise decision to avoid officially pinning the blame on one community or other and anyhow, the issue was far more the underlying community issues.

Both Mr Lee and Tun Razak did agree on how explosive the situation was – and how it could have become even more so unless urgent action was taken. Mr Lee had added in his broadcast: 'Right now, our business is to stop this stupidity. The vast majority of our people want to live in peace with each other. To them I make this appeal to stay indoors tonight and make easier the task of the police and the military in dealing with marauding groups who are out to make mischief.'

Tun Razak, in his radio appeal for calm, said: 'If we are divided, we shall all be destroyed. We must not be at odds with one another nor must we fight each other. If we fight one another, Malaysia will be destroyed and so will all of us.'

Brewing Tensions Beneath

Exactly who did trigger things off is, as noted, of comparatively lesser importance than the fact that the violence happened in the first place. Its background, its causes sprang from the micro-issue of the Geylang 'resettlements'. There was tension among Malays that their traditions and general way of doing things was being usurped by Singapore's mainly-Chinese government decision to turn Geylang into a modern satellite town with high-rise blocks of flats, involving the wholesale destruction of its many kampongs, little poultry farms, etc.

In 1963, Mr Lee had announced a $3.7 million plan to turn much of Geylang into a modern residential/shopping area, billing the project as a 'special social experiment to show if the Malays can take to flat dwellings'.

In August of that year, he laid the foundation stone for the first block in this Geylang redevelopment scheme – at which stage Malay suspicions of enforced cultural absorption were running high. For there were then an estimated 15,000 families and overall, 90,000 people living in the sprawling Geylang kampong zone bounded by today's Paya Lebar Road, Old Airport Road, Jalan Eunos and Changi Road, with almost all

Scorpion Orchid

The delicate and often turbulent state of Singapore's interracial relations during the 1950/60s formed the dramatic backdrop for Lloyd Fernando's 1976 novel *Scorpion Orchid*. He adapted his novel into a play with the same name, which was premiered by TheatreWorks during the Singapore Festival of Arts 1994.

its inhabitants being Malays and/or from various Indonesian strands who had mingled in what was called 'the melting pot of the Malay Archipelago'.

Adding further dry tinder to the potential fire was the macro-issue of Singapore's largely-unhappy federation within the new Malaysia, with all the questions this status raised about its Malay and Chinese citizens. Such as: Was Malaysia for the Malays? Was Singapore for the Chinese? Was a unified approach possible? Why were Kuala Lumpur politicians alleging that Singapore's government discriminated against the island's Malay population?

Furthermore, there were those rumbles from Jakarta that took violent shape in the form of Indonesia's Konfrontasi with this new 'Greater' Malaysia. One of its earliest ***Rumbles from Jakarta ...*** bombs exploded (significantly) at a newly-completed HDB block just off Changi Road in April 1964, killing two people. And Jakarta's agitating influence was detectable in the second racial flare-up which Geylang endured in September 1964.

Gay World Attacked

On the troubled night of 21 July after the gasworks incident, fighting broke out all along the procession's route to Geylang, such as when Chinese food hawkers in the Gay World complex on Geylang Road were attacked and had their stalls wrecked. The authorities acted fast. An area from Arab Street to Changi Road was cordoned off with barbed wire and with police guns at the ready, as word of the rioting spread around town and other areas 'joined in'. One such was North Bridge Road, soon littered with the debris of smashed cars and broken shop windows.

A strict overnight curfew was imposed that same evening, troops were rushed from Peninsular Malaysia, and those high-level appeals for calm were made repeatedly over the radio. But this 'forest fire' had not yet run its full destructive course.

Ahmad Mattar's Narrow Escape

One near-victim of Singapore's racial madness was Dr Ahmad Mattar, former Environment Minister. Driving on his way through early-morning town to Shenton Way, his new car was stopped by a big crowd of angry Chinese and when he got out, he heard one Chinese man shout at him the Hokkien word for 'attack'. Dr Mattar ran away as fast as his legs could carry him.

Recounting this incident in 1991 while talking about the menace of communalism, PM Mr Goh Chok Tong said: 'He (i.e. Mattar) fell down several times. He got up, he fell down again. His legs were stiff and cold, but he escaped. It was just after 7 am, so the crowd was not interested in chasing after him. But they burned his car.'

The tension did not die with the new day, and there were other incidents in various parts of the island (often rarely racial in origin, more like plain criminal behaviour, looting and the like). The atmosphere was captured by the words of a Beach Ròad resident who said: 'I watched as a goldsmith's shop was attacked by youths with acid. Everybody was preparing for a fight. After the curfew hours, when people went out to shop, my family bought waterpipes which we cut into points as weapons, and 44 gallon (200 litre) drums of acid to pour from the upstairs window in case anyone attacked.'

On 24 July, 263 people appeared in court, of whom 142 were sent to jail for terms varying from two days to two years. One group of 13 was charged with breaching the peace in Yio Chu Kang Road; two men got two years for rioting in Palmer Road; others faced charges of carrying offensive weapons. The most frequent offence was curfew-breaking.

Soon, reconciliation exercises were underway, with multiracial 'goodwill commissions' set up by Mr Lee who toured the major trouble spots to soothe fears and doubts – and anger.

Upon his hurried return from the US, Tunku Abdul Rahman also toured these Singapore trouble spots in the back of an open-topped jeep alongside Mr Lee, with both men issuing loudspeaker appeals.

Singapore had learned – if at a costly price – essential lessons in racial sensitivities at both the highest political level and at the grassroots level of neighbours who had never even talked to each other before. They had kept within their racial affiliations, but now they gingerly opened up and (surprisingly?) found that their basic worries and concerns were shared by all – be they Malays, Chinese or whoever.

The underlying troublesome issue of the Geylang resettlements was soothed by a very different sort of outbreak later in that turning-point year of 1964.

In September, heavy rains caused the worst flooding Geylang had seen in living memory. Excrement, rubbish, filth and all **Worst floods in living memory ...** sorts floated through the lanes and under the kampong houses, making Geylang both look and smell like a huge and deeply unpleasant slum, full of menace to health and wealth. So suddenly it was the poor drainage, sanitation and overcrowding that struck local residents as the more important issues, rather than threats to traditional ways of life.

By the next year, the first blocks of new Geylang flats were ready and 4,000 people had moved in. One early Malay HDB resident was quoted as saying: 'I had a spanking clean flat with no mosquitoes and a toilet that flushed.' The Geylang home-building continued at a fast pace, with the very last kampong dwellers leaving (for a modern Hougang flat) in 1980.

A Hari Raya Wonderland

These days, Geylang is still the centre of Singapore Malayness. Never more so than the annual Hari Raya season, when the roads around Geylang Serai market are lit up and brightly decorated. That market retains its Malay nature, with visitors

Every Hari Raya Puasa sees Geylang transformed into a paradise of festive goodies.

from Malaysia and Indonesia making their way there to admire its fabrics and materials (for making *baju kurung, baju kebaya, kain songket,* etc), its foodstuffs, its bargains, the deliberate absence of pork from its wet market, its general atmosphere and opportunity to catch up with old friends.

That word 'serai' means 'lemon grass', pointing to the farming pursuits that ruled in this part of town, east of the Geylang river when it was a collection of kampongs with stilt-houses and attap roofs. The street names around the market point further to the area's past: Ubi (tapioca); Keladi (spinach); Bayam (spinach); Kobis (cabbage); and Kelapa (coconut). And the word Geylang itself? This is widely thought to have derived from the word 'kelang', meaning factory – which yes, is disappointingly prosaic.

But what to do with Geylang's Malay Village on its 1.76 ha site bounded by Geylang Serai, Sims Avenue and Geylang Road? The idea first arose in August 1984 from a group of Malay MPs who felt it right that this part of Singapore should have a lasting memorial to its traditional Malayness. Costing some $8 million to create, the Malay Village had its (delayed) grand opening in February 1990.

With its declared intentions of showcasing Malay craft-making, top-spinning, kite-flying, batik-printing, ceremonial Malay weddings, *silat* arts of self-defence and the like, the complex fits in well with a plastic Singaporean approach to its heritage – 'theme-parkology'. Yet the Malay Village is still having trouble in standing on its own (economic) feet, despite its delightful visuals and splendid Malacca-style tiled central twin-pronged staircase at its Singgahsana Hall.

More recently, it has switched to that surefire Singaporean attraction of food, with its on-stilts Restoran Temenggung where diners can allegedly 'savour authentic Malay cuisine in a kampong ambience' and its Stargazer food court. Nevertheless, most local people going to Geylang still prefer the lively, more atmospheric reality of Geylang's markets, foodstalls, Joo Chiat Complex, City Plaza and so on to the pricey charms of the Malay Village.

However, memories of those awful six days when Geylang was the epicentre of the racial madness that rocked Singapore have not been completely forgotten. For old resentments rushed back to the surface following the publication of *The Singapore Story: Memoirs of Lee Kuan Yew* (volume one) in September 1998 to mark the Senior Minister's 75th birthday. In this, Mr Lee gave his pugnacious version of how the 1964 race riots exploded – and this provoked public responses from those in Malaysia who put a different spin on those turbulent times some 35 years ago. Enough to suggest that this unhappy chapter has still not been finally laid to rest.

The Rest of
the Island

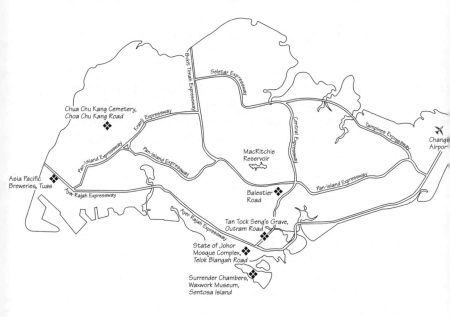

Chua Chu Kang Cemetery,
Choa Chu Kang Road

Bukit Timah Expressway

Seletar Expressway

Kranji Expressway

Pan-Island Expressway

Pan-Island Expressway

Central Expressway

Tampines Expressway

Changi
Airport

MacRitchie
Reservoir

Asia Pacific
Breweries, Tuas

Ayer Rajah Expressway

Pan-Island Expressway

Balestier
Road

Ayer Rajah Expressway

Tan Tock Seng's Grave,
Outram Road

State of Johor
Mosque Complex,
Telok Blangah Road

Surrender Chambers,
Waxwork Museum,
Sentosa Island

For Whom the Bells Toll

Joseph Balestier, Singapore's first American Consul
Balestier Road

Joseph Balestier, Singapore's first American Consul,
had to work from neighbouring Bintan island for two
years, all because of a diplomatic slip-of-the-pen ...

Joseph Balestier could well still be the most significant American to tread Singapore's soil (even if Michael Jackson did get more publicity). For Balestier left behind his name, all over the old postal district 1232. While his wife left behind a rather big bell, even if it does now lie cracked and soundless in the National Museum.

From this historical distance, Balestier seemed to do things the hard way. In 1834, he was appointed American Consul in Singapore by US President Andrew Jackson. Only he could not perform his duties of office in Singapore itself; he had to work from the island of Bintan, with his office in Tanjung Pinang. The reason for this was intriguing. It was because of a British navy officer whose slavish devotion to his perceived duty evokes those Japanese soldiers still in the jungles of Sarawak or wherever who refused to accept that their war ended in 1945.

In 1825, this navy officer was at the helm of British warship HMS Larne. He ordered his crew to board, then impound an American ship called Governor Endicott while it was harmlessly making its way down through the Strait of Malacca for Singapore. Instead of Boat Quay, Endicott was ordered to sail to Calcutta (then the city which administered Singapore).

There, the Larne's skipper pleaded that the 1815 settlement of the Britain-US war had listed all the British ports at which US ships were now permitted to trade. As Singapore was (absent-mindedly) omitted from this list, the naval officer considered it to be still in a state of war with the US. In an ultra-bureaucratic way, he was correct. In reality no one else was paying much attention to this slip-of-the-pen quirk.

The Larne's skipper was scolded in Calcutta for being so pedantic but in Washington DC, diplomatic damage had been done. American ships were ordered to avoid Singapore and use Bintan (then administered by the Netherlands) when in the area. There American boats would wait for Singapore traders to cross to them, and there Joseph Balestier had to sail every day to perform his proper duties as Consul.

It took 10 years for this silly diplomatic statement to be resolved, and not till 1836 was Balestier able to begin the first official US representation on Singaporean soil.

A New England Farmer in the Tropics

Dubbed a 'much-loved New Englander', Balestier had extensive business interests in Singapore but decided to throw his money into agriculture. He took over 1,000 acres of swamp- and tiger-infested jungle that was soon called Balestier Plain. He used elephants, Thai-style, to help clear the land of its trees, insisting that he would there grow sugar.

Balestier's first problem came with his contracted Chinese workforce, who were rightly alarmed at the tigers that prowled the estate. The *Free Press* newspaper reported (in a strangely jolly way) on a November 1843 incident on Balestier Plain thus:

'... a Chinaman was pounced upon by a tiger who, after killing him and sucking the blood, walked into the jungle leaving the body behind. We suppose the tiger, knowing the object of the Chinaman's labours (he had been digging a tiger-pit), took the opportunity of giving a striking manifestation of his profound disapproval of all such latent and unfair methods of putting an enemy at a disadvantage.'

Great Bells!

The world's largest uncracked bell is in Burma, at Mingun just north of Mandalay. This weighs 90 tonnes, smaller only than the (cracked) Great Bell in Moscow's Kremlin. Singapore's copper/iron Revere Bell measures 89 cm in diameter, stands 81 cm high, and weighs about one tonne. During the National Museum's renovation in 1990, even 10 men could not move it.

Balestier finally got his land cleared and even built canals that could float his hoped-for sugar down to the harbour for export. Alas, he found that what everyone had warned him was true: the red soil of Singapore would not profitably take to sugar cane production.

Plus his land was notoriously ***Tragedy strikes ...*** unhealthy and mosquito-ridden. Tragically, there his son died and in 1847, so did his wife. Mrs Balestier had the maiden name Maria Revere and was indeed the daughter of that noted figure in the US Revolutionary War against the British. For Paul Revere undertook those famous midnight horse rides in April 1775 through the streets of Boston to warn: 'The British are coming!'

Paul Revere was also a noted bell-maker. In 1843, Mrs Balestier presented one of her father's noted bells to St Andrew's Cathedral – on one condition. That it sounded an evening curfew, just five minutes after the regular 8 pm firing of a government cannon on Fort Canning Hill.

This bell went to the military church in Tanglin barracks in 1911 but soon, it cracked and could chime no more. It was kept in the National Museum during the 1930s and now bears the proud boast that it is the only 'Revere Bell' outside the US, a fact which usually impresses visiting Americans. Maria Revere,

> **Crime of Passion**
>
> Balestier Road can claim a distinction, as a murder in one of its shophouses in December 1880 (of her husband) led to the first hanging in Singapore of a Chinese woman. She swung together with her lover; both had been convicted on the evidence of her eldest son.

who was clearly not a woman for night-time frolics, lies buried in the Fort Canning Christian cemetery.

In 1847, heavy rains and poor drainage flooded out Balestier Plain and, with his own health failing, Joseph called it a day by declaring himself bankrupt. In April 1848, the estate was put up for sale as an ongoing sugar plantation although it had proved itself anything but.

Joseph Balestier himself quite understandably finally left Singapore behind in 1848, returning to the US where his health recovered and he lived a long life. It could further be noted that this would-be sugar baron was a founder member of the Singapore Chamber of Commerce. And that his town house, at the junction of Stamford and North Bridge roads, became the noted Seamen's Hospital cum lodging house (where novelist Joseph Conrad recovered from the illness that first brought him to Singapore) before in due course making way for the art deco Capitol cinema complex.

A Hospital is Born

The sadly neglected grave of the man
who founded Tan Tock Seng Hospital
*The grassy slope next to Jubilee Church,
256 Outram Road*

In 1844, Singapore's first 'rags-to-riches' Chinese
tycoon set up a much-needed hospital for the poor.

Tan Tock Seng's impressive grave stands alone on the grassy
embankment above an Outram Road bus-stop. Alone, that
is, bar four small stone dragons which stand solemn guard.

Unnoticed by many, Tock Seng's grave with its Chinese
red lettering was 'rediscovered' during the first national
Heritage Hunt in 1988. After which Mr Tay Kheng Soon,
chairman of the Heritage Committee, was moved to comment:
'This is a clear case where the Preservation of Monuments Board
should do something. He was a man of great importance and
should be given due respect. His tomb should be kept and
maintained, and a plaque should be put up describing his
achievements.'

This was the second time in recent years that the grave
commanded respect. For when Outram Road was being
widened, the intention was to shift Tan Tock Seng's remains
elsewhere. But a descendant named Tan Teck Chuan (a lawyer)
pleaded a successful case for leaving the grave alone, given
the contribution the man had made to early Singapore's quality
of life. And so, the road widening stopped just short of the
grave.

Tan Tock Seng, a Hokkien born in Malacca in 1798, came
to the new Singapore in 1819 and proved to be the first local
'rags-to-riches' Chinese success story. He started off by selling
vegetables, fruit and poultry, going into the thick inland jungle
to buy the produce he would then sell in town.

In 1827, he opened his own shop on Boat Quay, then started
making his serious money through property acquisition and

speculation (such as with the Ellenborough buildings and market off North Bridge Road).

He became the first Asian magistrate here, a benefactor of the 1839 Thian Hock Keng temple on Telok Ayer Street – and in 1844, the founder of the hospital which still bears his name.

A Poor House in Bras Basah

Singapore's public healthcare in the 1840s consisted solely of a small, attap-roofed shed on what is today's Bras Basah Park. This was meant for those too poor to hire a private doctor's services and soon became known as the Poor House. There was no other healthcare for those Chinese and other non-whites (the majority) who had proved unable to enact their own Singapore success stories, and whom the European overlords felt no compulsion to help them out.

They would need a 'look after our own' gesture from prosperous Chinese merchants, such as Tan Tock Seng. As the *Free Press* newspaper of January 1844 reported, when his bequest became known: 'We are glad to learn that there is now every chance of a suitable hospital for the reception of diseased and aged Chinese paupers being erected, and what is still more gratifying, chiefly through the means of the Chinese themselves.

'A number of diseased Chinese, lepers and others frequent almost every street in town, presenting a spectacle which is rarely to be met with, even in towns under a pagan government, and which is truly disgraceful in a civilised and Christian country, especially under the government of Englishmen.'

The island's Calcutta-based administration of the time was being pressured to fund a proper European sailors' hospital also, as ship captains would often simply dump ill and thus unwanted sailors in Singapore, leaving them to cope as best they could.

Governor Butterworth implored Calcutta to impose a hospital-building tax (an early idea was 2% on pork) to support the hospital being set up by Tan Tock Seng's generous $7,000 donation. Tock Seng himself felt he could not wait for 'official approval' and on 25 May 1844, the foundation stone of the Chinese Pauper Hospital Singapore (though meant for 'the diseased of all nations') was laid on a Pearl's Hill site – close to where, during the same year, the European Seaman's Hospital would also start up.

By 1852 (two years after Tan Tock Seng's own death at the age of 52), his hospital was full to the rafters. The *Free Press* noted: 'For some time past, the patients admitted into

Full to the rafters ...
Tan Tock Seng's hospital have been far more numerous than there are any means of accommodating, and the consequence has been a great overcrowding, so that the diseases of the patients – instead of being alleviated – have in fact been aggravated by their reception into the hospital.'

Tan's son, Kim Cheng, stepped in and donated a further $2,000 to build a hospital extension. But the Indian Mutiny of 1857 put a stop to any more public spending in Singapore and what's more, required that those hospital buildings on Pearl's Hill be taken over for military purposes.

Moving to Balestier Plain

The European Hospital was booted out to the race course grounds (today's Kandang Kerbau Hospital being the 'descendant' of this enforced transfer) while Tan Tock Seng's hospital went to swampy Balestier Plain.

Soon, 400 paupers were crowded into the new Tan Tock Seng Hospital. It rapidly became a public disgrace, an embarrassment to health officials. One such, Dr Joseph Rose (the island's Senior Medical Officer), refused to take visitors near the place, appalled as he was at its overcrowding and its poor drainage, caused by that waterlogged Balestier Plain.

Its food was in short supply, too, as more patients meant less food to go around each day. Among the benefactors sending food supplies there was Thomas Dunman, the

European who set up Singapore's first proper police force. He sent the slaughtered fighting cocks his men had confiscated during raids on illegal cockpits.

The average death rate at this hospital was two a day, not helped by the dirty, miserable shed in which lepers were herded. By the 1880s, the hospital had become an out-and-out scandal. In 1898, an outbreak of beri-beri took hold, adding to the pressure being put on the Colonial Office in London to authorise spending on a proper hospital.

An out-and-out scandal ...

The main problem was that swampy, unhealthy Balestier Plain. As the early Singapore chronicler C.A. Buckley noted: 'This should have been the last place to be chosen for the purpose.' Buckley quoted statistics showing that 'the germs of disease were so rampant in the hospital, that those who came in for treatment for one complaint died in the hospital from another they contracted in it.'

Onward to Moulmein Road

The breakthrough came in 1909. Tan Tock Seng Hospital moved for the third time – this time, to its current location on Moulmein Road. It now had 16 dormitory wards in well-designed, healthy buildings costing some $500,000 to construct. Alongside it was Middleton Hospital, a quarantine camp for the dangerous infectious diseases of the time such as smallpox, cholera and typhoid, until its 1985 merger with Tan Tock Seng Hospital and its new name as the Communicable Disease Centre.

The spanking new $580-million Tan Tock Seng Hospital opened fully for business on the same off-Moulmein Road site in May 1999, with 1,211 beds in 34 wards – all housed in four linked blocks, including a showpiece 14-storey tower block. As one long-serving Tan Tock Seng medical staff member put it: 'Now we won't have to carry umbrellas or cross a road to get from one block to another. At the new hospital, it is all under one roof.'

No doubt it will still be known by many Chinese-speakers as the 'Black Lion' hospital, after the distinctive logo on its Moulmein Road front entrance gate. And it will still preserve the historic early Tan Tock Seng foundation stones, telling the details of his $5,000 donation (and that of his son Kim Cheng) for 'the diseased of all nations'.

The Sultans from Telok Blangah

State of Johor Mosque Complex
Telok Blangah Road

Here lies the grand tomb of Temenggong Abdul Rahman,
whose descendants would make the leap from seafaring
pirates to the throne of modern Johor ...

It's a quiet cluster of small buildings on Telok Blangah Road,
right opposite the exhibition halls of the World Trade Centre
and close to Sentosa's landbridge.

So easy to miss, this complex has such a
story to tell. A story that predates the 1819
Raffles arrival, that evokes the 18th century
era when Singapore was just a sleepy outpost

*So easy
to miss ...*

of the Johor-Riau empire. A story that parallels the 19th century
growth of Singapore and the 'opening out' of the state of Johor.
A story that is a rather long one ...

For this Telok Blangah complex is, along with Istana
Kampong Glam, the historical centre of the Malay tradition
in Singapore and its adaptation to the acceleration of change
brought to the island by its British development and the
subsequent influx of Chinese immigrants.

The complex was much bigger once. Now its focal point is
its mosque, a new building which cost S$1.6 million and was
opened in 1993 to replace a mosque that had stood here for
over 130 years. Behind is a building that once served as a
reception hall for those visiting a rather grand istana a little
higher up the hill. It's long since disappeared but traces remain
in the form of brickwork that once enclosed the royal baths,
fed by a fresh water stream.

One more building is here – a shrine known as Tanah Kubor
Raja. Its centrepiece is the grand tomb of Abdul Rahman,
covered with yellow silk. Rahman was the Temenggong (a royal

appointment, roughly meaning 'chieftain') of the Johor-Riau Malay kingdom that included Singapore – and the man with whom Raffles did business in 1819.

His relatives lie close by, forming a direct family line to the current Sultan of Johor who pays an annual visit here in tribute to his ancestors. It's a family line that reflects the rapid development of the indigenous Malay population: from seafaring 'pirates' caught up in the imperial contest between the British and the Dutch, through to the modern affluence and independence of Johor.

Where It All Began ...

To trace this line, we must time-travel back to the 1700s when the region's seat of power and influence was Bintan island.

In the 1700s, this region's crude economy was sea-based. That is, trading and what both the early British and Dutch regarded as piracy. Or the extraction of tribute due for the use of their waters, as the Malay chieftains saw it.

In 1784, the Dutch attacked Bintan and disrupted the Malay chain of command. In 1806, Abdul Rahman became Temenggong but he failed to establish undisputed control of either the economy or political power in the Johor-Riau axis. And when the Dutch returned in 1818 to formally incorporate Bintan and the other Riau islands within their East Indies empire, they chose to favour Rahman's internal enemies, casting him into the political wilderness.

But not for long. In January 1819, Stamford Raffles and William Farquhar pulled into the Singapore river. Using the well-tested British colonial tactic of divide-and-rule, they played upon Rahman's injured pride and in the treaty they signed with him, they recognised him as the 'Ruler of Singapore, who governs the country of Singapore in his own name and in the name of Sree Sultan Hussein'. And on behalf of the British East India Company, of course.

Sultan Hussein (Rahman's political enemy) was then hastily sent for by the British, and given the nominal position of power in Singapore. But it was the Temenggong who had effective control, much like the status in a modern state of a President and a Prime Minister. Following this new agreement in 1819, the old Malay kingdom of Johor-Riau ceased to exist. A line had been drawn across its centre (through the Singapore Strait) and the modern history of this region had begun.

Acts of Piracy

At first the Temenggong and his followers (some 600 of them) occupied an area that now has Parliament House at its centre, an area Raffles had decreed was for government purposes. In British eyes, the Malays were soon causing nothing but trouble. They fought in the streets with their rivals, Malaccan Malays who had followed Farquhar to Singapore, and offshore they engaged in 'acts of piracy' which rather spoilt the central British concept of running Singapore as an open, duty-free port for all who cared to trade there.

Plus the Temenggong's men were costing the British a lot, what with their annual $3,000 Spanish silver dollars allowance from the East India Company. In 1823, they were demanding more from Raffles, refusing his alternative suggestion that they become merchants and traders, thereby taking part in young Singapore's rapid growth. Rahman sneered: 'It is not the custom of rulers to engage in trade, for they would lose dignity.'

British patience quickly came to an end. The 1819 Treaty's formal recognition of Malay rule was drawn up that way only because by being 'constitutional', Raffles felt he would circumvent Dutch objections and possible military intervention.

Then in 1824, London and Amsterdam came to a new agreement which gave Malacca to the British in return for all its footholds in what is now Indonesia; this agreement also officially ended Dutch hostility towards a British Singapore. Thus there was no longer any political need to keep the Temenggong sweet.

A new treaty was drawn up in August 1824, with the Temenggong and Sultan being forced to surrender all claims to **A new treaty ...** ownership of Singapore and to make a pledge to 'suppress piracy', all in return for a single cash payment and increased 'pensions'. In 1818, Rahman had lost out in Bintan. Now in 1824, he had lost out in Singapore.

He was next forced to move his men away from the swelling town centre, with the then Resident John Crawfurd insisting they were 'a nuisance of the first magnitude'. Before the end of that year, the whole kampong had been shifted due west to an 'ulu' 200-acre site in Telok Blangah between the seafront and the tip of what is now Mount Faber. In effect, they were out of sight and out of mind. This indignity was slightly soothed by a 'moving expenses' cash payment of $6,000.

In 1825, a broken Abdul Rahman died. His was the first burial in the Telok Blangah royal shrine.

His son Daing Ibrahim was just 15 in 1825, too young an age to become Temenggong himself. But his cause was helped when his technical superior Sultan Hussein left Singapore in 1834, also a dispirited man, to die in Malacca two years later.

Ibrahim's youth meant camp followers drifted away, despite his assumption in the early 1830s of the Temenggong title. Some of them settled in Batam/Bintan, some in Johor, and most of them resumed their sea piracy. Or, from *orang laut* to *bajak laut* (sea pirates) again.

A Unflattering Portrait of Ibrahim

In 1835, then Resident George Bonham painted an unflattering picture of Ibrahim: 'Idle and completely illiterate; indeed, except by his clothes and consequent personal appearance, not a remove higher on the scale of civilisation than the meanest of his followers.'

Despite these insults, Bonham made it his business in 1836 to deal with Ibrahim and got his 'permission' to suppress that growing piracy around the waters of Singapore. This proved a crucial political breakthrough for Ibrahim, as he turned these new links with the British authorities to his own advantage.

During 1837, British gunboats combed the waters around the nearby Riau islands, blasting out of the sea any vessel they took to be manned by 'pirates'. This drove seafaring Malays back to Singapore, where they again sought the Temenggong's protection. In return, they paid him allegiance and helped the restoration of his status.

This received a further boost in 1837 when the first of the big British traders moved docking facilities to the Telok Blangah seafront. This was then becoming a valuable stretch of real estate, no longer the 'nowhere-land' of just 13 years before.

For the Singapore river was proving too small as a harbour for rapidly increasing boat traffic, and the deep channel of the New Harbour (today's Keppel Harbour) was the obvious alternative. Soon traders such as James Guthrie bought land off the Temenggong and by 1845, the mighty P&O Navigation Company had opened up a steamship link with Singapore, using that New Harbour.

With good income heading back his way, Ibrahim was proving lucky. There had been no Sultan since Hussein's death in 1836. Hussein's son Tengku Ali had gained the title of Sultan of Johor but in 1855, with British approval, he signed away his rights over Singapore-Johor to Ibrahim in return for a cash payment.

The Tragic Tale of Radin Mas

Telok Blangah ('Cooking Pot Bay' in Malay) was not all serenity in its early days; some extremely dramatic local dramas took place here. Such as the arrival of the teenaged Radin Mas ('Golden Princess') with her father, after he had fled from Java where his brother (a ruling Sultan) had killed the princess' mother for being a mere 'commoner'.

Father and daughter settled into the Telok Blangah community but when he married one of the Temenggong's daughters, ill fortune returned. The stepmother proved a horror, tormenting her father (by, it is said, imprisoning him in a well) and forcing Radin Mas into an unwanted marriage. On the big day, fearing vengeance for the stepmother's ill-treatment, the princess' would-be groom tried to stab her father with his kris. Radin Mas threw herself in the way, receiving a fatal stab wound in the self-denying process.

Other Telok Blangah villagers had come to love the sweet princess, so they built her a tomb which still stands today in a little grove behind Mount Faber Lodge condo. Her name – Radin Mas – has also lived on; it is now the charming name of a Parliamentary constituency in this area.

Cash Ibrahim was short of, mainly because he was no longer officially practising piracy. The rubber-like gutta-percha was plentiful in the thick tropical Johor forests and was being cultivated, though only for small items like riding whips. One such whip found its way back to London in the 1840s and caused great excitement among the boffins of the Royal Asiatic Society.

Great excitement in London ...

Gutta-Percha Makes Golf History

In 1992, a rare golf ball described as 'the missing link in golfing history', was sold at a London auction for S$17,400! It was one of the very first golf balls made from Johor's 'miracle' gutta-percha, which replaced leather golf balls stuffed with feathers.

A Thriving Export Business

They realised that gutta-percha was the ideal (tougher than rubber) material to insulate the first seabed telegraph cables that were being laid about this time. Soon, most of Europe and the US was demanding Johor's supplies for all sorts of things – up to and including golf balls.

Ibrahim claimed a personal monopoly over Johor's gutta-percha; Singapore's British authorities did not object. Official British recognition of the change in Ibrahim's status from a decrepit outcast pirate into a respected landowner and commodity-dealer came in 1846. At a special Government Hill ceremony, Governor Butterworth presented the Temenggong with a Sword of Honour to note his efforts in stopping the piracy, the piracy he had once controlled.

Ibrahim had become an influential and wealthy man through dealing with, rather than opposing, the British presence in Singapore. In 1855, Ibrahim set about grooming his successor, his 20-year-old son Abu Bakar, to continue Johor's good fortune.

Ibrahim died in 1862 and was buried alongside his uncle in Tanah Kubor Raja at Telok Blangah. Abu Bakar was by then well-versed in business affairs and perfectly comfortable in his dealings with British and Chinese interests, ready to become an able Temenggong. His father had laid the groundwork for his and Johor's wealth. Abu Bakar took it from there. In 1866, he travelled to London and met Queen Victoria, building up

> ## Johor Bahru – A City for the Future
>
> In 1855, what's now known as Johor Bahru was founded by Ibrahim, under the name Iskandar Putri (it got its current name in 1866). Ibrahim's son Abu Bakar shifted Johor's administration away from Telok Blangah and across the Strait of Johor. On New Year's Day 1994, Johor Bahru was at last proclaimed a city and enjoyed 48 hours' worth of festivities to celebrate the civic occasion.

direct personal links with the British government, which meant he could often go over the heads of the power represented by the occupant of Singapore's Government House.

During another London visit, it was noted about Abu Bakar: 'He lived as a young man half in the traditional Malay world and half in the world of a cosmopolitan British port.' He travelled around other countries in Europe, effectively mounting a diplomatic 'charm offensive' to serve his own interests and gain influence in the Old World.

A diplomatic 'charm offensive' ...

With Sir Harry Ord becoming the first British Governor of Singapore in 1868, the Europeanisation of Abu Bakar paid off. Ord paid him a fulsome public tribute: 'In his tastes and habits, he is an English gentleman. As a ruler he is ... the only Rajah in the whole peninsula and surrounding territories who rules in accordance with the practice of civilised nations.'

In just one generation, Abu Bakar's family line had 'matured' from piratical outsiders to respected administrators on the inside fast-track.

Sultan Abu Bakar at Last

Abu Bakar's burning desire for Sultan status reaped its reward in 1885, just a few years after Istana Kampong Glam's Sultan

Let There be Light – and Fire

The Sultan was one of the very first in Singapore to have his home lit up by electricity. He had his own generating station installed within Tyersall's grounds, and his 1892 party guests were dazzled by the lavishness of the chandeliers that so brightened up the palace.

Alas, that newfangled electricity was the reason why the building has fared so poorly in the 20th century. Faulty wiring was blamed for a fire in September 1905 which so badly damaged the palace, it was abandoned by the Sultan, though he still owns its land and the ample surrounding grounds off Holland Road.

Tengku Ali died, leaving no suitable heir. Abu travelled (yet again) to London, this time to sign a new Treaty with the Colonial Office in which he was officially recognised as Sultan. His official title was Sultan of the State and Territory of Johor.

Abu Bakar was not, as he had secretly hoped, made Sultan of all Malaya. Plus the British side made it plain that Johor's foreign affairs were strictly a London matter. Nonetheless, Abu Bakar now had his desired title – and it inspired him into setting out to make Johor 'the greatest Malay power, to keep her free and to make her rich'.

Telok Blangah had by now been more-or-less abandoned. In Johor, the new Sultan strove to diversify its agriculture and attract European investment while continuing his diplomacy – which naturally meant he could indulge his acquired taste for globetrotting. In 1889–90, he could be spotted within the aristocratic circles of Cairo, Athens, Istanbul and Vienna where, it was noted, he 'cut a great dash' (being considered a rather exotic Eastern figure).

It was also noted that his wanderings were costing the new State of Johor's Treasury rather a lot of money. What's more,

Abu Bakar built himself a palace at Tyersall in Singapore, plus ones in Johor Bahru and in Muar, too.

The splendid Tyersall palace in its 67 acres of grounds was declared open on 10 December 1892 with a grand bash. According to the *Singapore Free Press*: 'Seldom has a more numerous gathering of Singapore society been seen ... the Sultan was resplendent in diamonds.'

The occasion was arranged also to celebrate the Sultan receiving the Order of the Double Dragon (First Class) from the Emperor of China, in recognition of the 'kindness' shown by the government of Johor towards 'the numerous subjects of the Chinese Empire dwelling within its territory'.

In response, the Sultan remarked that the Chinese had done so much for his country 'it was no exaggeration to say that, without them, Johor would never have become what it was. It might even have ceased to exist at all.'

A True-Blue English Gentleman

In his turn, Abu Bakar groomed his son (also called Ibrahim) for the succession by bringing him up as a true English gentleman, interested in sport and military concerns rather than in commerce or trade. He once gave his son a piece of cynical advice before introducing him to some real English gentlemen. He was overheard to say in Malay: 'If you can't talk sense, talk nonsense. Only talk plenty.'

'If you can't talk sense, talk nonsense ...

Abu Bakar died in London in 1895, before rubber and palm oil plantations replaced the gambier, pepper and gutta-percha trees of his state, enabling its prosperity to continue and the expensive royal way of life to flourish. His son Ismail would reign as Sultan until 1959 in what was one of the world's longest royal reigns.

Common folk can now enthuse over royal Johor's bric-a-brac (gathered worldwide) in a splendid museum that opened

> ### Different Strokes in Kampong Glam
>
> Many 'rival' Malays in Kampong Glam were unimpressed with the rapid social advancement achieved by the upwardly-mobile Telok Blangah clan. A disrespectful song had a verse which went: 'The gaudy lantern is bound in rattan/Humble kemmuning wood holds the kris/The Temenggong has become a Sultan/Though his royal forbears are the Bugis.' It rhymes in the original Malay, too.

in May 1990. This is called the Royal Abu Bakar Museum and is sited within Johor Bahru's charming Istana Besar complex.

This museum is effectively an authentication of the royal Johor line. Inside, it presents its own interpretation of local history. It bewails the handing over of Singapore island to the British in 1819, which it describes as 'a surrender' helped by 'deceitful agreements' forced by the British on the 'weak' Johor sultanate of the time.

Deceitful agreements ...

Royal Trouble Across the Causeway

The current Sultan of Johor Mahmood Iskandar served his turn as a popular King of all Malaysia but then found himself the spark that fired off much Malaysian government-royalty ill-will during 1992–93 (it was basically about KL wanting royalty to keep out of politics).

Many astonishing stories of royal acts of misconduct emerged in Malaysia's newspapers, following a public outcry over an alleged assault on a Johor school hockey coach (not to mention extraordinary allegations from the golf course).

The upshot was that in January 1993, the Malaysian Parliament passed a bill to strip the nation's nine Sultans of

Mesjid Temenggung Daing Ibrahim Johor Darul Ta'zim today.

their legal immunity. Details of the handsome allowances paid to all the royal families then emerged (and such juicy tidbits as how many tax-free luxury cars the various Sultans owned), causing much rubbing in disbelief of the public's eyes. And Malaysian Prime Minister Dr Mahathir issued a stern warning to 'errant' Sultans: 'If he is not suitable and if he likes to beat people and so on, we should consider if he is fit to be a ruler.'

In Johor, where the 'commoners' backlash' started, it was announced that state spending on the Sultan's eight palaces would be cut and that his controversial 'private army', the 195-strong Johor Military Force, might be disbanded.

As noted so very long ago, that small and easily-overlooked cluster of buildings opposite WTC's exhibition halls has ever such a tale to tell. And the full Malay name of its mosque is also long: Mesjid Temenggung Daing Ibrahim Johor Darul Ta'zim.

A Waxwork Model

General Tomoyuki Yamashita
Surrender Chambers, Waxwork Museum, Sentosa

*On waxwork show in Sentosa is the mastermind behind
Japan's crushing victory over the 'impregnable fortress'
of Singapore in 1942 …*

General Tomoyuki Yamashita is that chunky bulldog of a
man on waxwork show at Sentosa's Surrender Chamber,
accepting the 'we give up' signature he had demanded on 15
February 1942 from Singapore's British commander Lt Gen A.
E. Percival. Two hours after this signing, seven days of fighting

Kranji Beach Horror

Kranji Beach proved to be the final stage at which
Yamashita's marauding army could have been kept off
Singaporean soil. At midnight on 9 February 1942 (in a
ferocious beach battle evoking Spielberg's *Saving Private
Ryan*), the 27th Australian Brigade with local Dalforce
irregulars stopped the invading Japanese in their tracks.
Aiming to slip in via Kranji river, the Japanese got bogged
down in mangrove swamps, following which the defending
forces demolished fuel tanks, poured the oil into the river
and set it ablaze. Many Japanese burnt to death in this
sea of fire, while barges carrying more troops across from
Johore were raked by deadly Australian machine gunfire.

Muddled orders, however, saw the 27th Brigade in
'strategic' retreat — and by the early hours of that Sunday,
the Japanese 5th Division had won its first significant
Singapore foothold. From Kranji, they fired off a
prearranged 'we've made it' red star shellburst towards
the Sultan of Johore's palace tower across the narrow strait,
where Yamashita was anxiously watching out for the signal.
These peaceful Sundays, Kranji Beach is full of amateur
fishermen, children at play and family picnic outings. A
National Heritage Board plaque here tells the story of a
very different kind of Sunday on Kranji Beach in 1942 …

The Surrender Room

The boardroom of the old Ford Motor Factory at 351 Upper Bukit Timah Road (by its 14 km point), where the British surrender document was signed on 15 February 1942 is miraculously still there and still intact, if more by neglect than by design. And it will be preserved as the unique historical site it is. Hong Leong is developing the land for swish condos but has pledged to preserve the Surrender Room within the overall design, possibly with a little museum attached.

In February 1992, Singapore marked the 50th anniversary of the Japanese invasion by opening up this Surrender Room to the public, which responded in their hundreds by visiting this real and non-themepark slice of local history. Not that the room looks anything special; just a musty, basic kind of space and much like an old schoolroom. Most of its furniture is 'authentic replacement'; the original table over which the two sides faced each other is now in Australia's official war museum in Canberra.

That Singapore is preserving and respecting the integrity of this room is a wise, mature decision. As Australian war historian Ian Ward put it, the old boardroom is the 'most important structure in Southeast Asia. I don't think you can underplay the historical significance of the building ...'

In a personal assurance to the author (March 1993), BG (NS) George Yeo, Minister of Information and the Arts, wrote: 'The Surrender Room at the old Ford Factory will be conserved.' It's still just about there now, hemmed in between Hong Leong's The Hillside condo and the sprawling Parc Palais apartments. But it's looking in pretty poor shape ...

on Singapore came to a sudden halt, the island was renamed Syonan-To – and the British Empire had suffered a crushing blow from which it was never to recover.

Yamashita quickly became known as the 'Tiger of Malaya' for the way his 25th Army had swept its conquering path (if often on bicycles) down the whole length of Malaya to reach

*The old factory may have gone but its boardroom where Percival
surrendered to Yamashita is still there.*

the 'impregnable fortress' of Singapore. All this in just 70 days
after Japanese troops had landed on the beaches of Kota Bharu,
Singora and Patani in the northeast corner of the Malayan
peninsula on 8 December 1941.

Penang had fallen on 16 December, Ipoh on 28 December,
Kuala Lumpur on 11 January, with the Allied forces retreating
to 'Fortress Singapore' on 31 January while Japanese forces
regrouped around Johor Bahru for their final assault. Before
Yamashita, the British and their allies had, as he put it, 'collapsed
in a moment, like a fan without a rivet'. And with the mocking
Malay words 'Orang putih lari' ringing in their ears – 'The
white men are running'.

An Audacious Bluff

Singapore was Yamashita's greatest military triumph. Even if,
as he noted in his diary, the British surrender was achieved
through 'a bluff that worked'. By which he meant that his 60,000
Japanese troops were confronted by over 130,000 Allied troops
on the island; his men were short of supplies and ammunition;
and that had the Allies mounted a more dogged defence, the

Where's the Surrender Document?

In January 1992, the Singapore Heritage Society launched a hunt for the actual surrender documents of 1942. But it emerged that the Japanese one had been burnt by Tokyo's War Ministry at war's end, while the British copy had simply 'gone missing'.

overstretched Japanese war machine could have been pushed back across the Johor Strait.

Yamashita put it this way: 'I was afraid in my heart that they would discover that our forces were much less than theirs. That was why I decided that I must use all means to make them surrender without terms.' This was in response to internal criticism that he had offended officers' etiquette by 'bullying and shouting at' General Percival.

Yamashita certainly came across as one mean dude. His final threat to Percival was: 'If you violate these terms, *One mean dude ...* the Japanese troops will waste no time in launching a general and final offensive against Singapore city.' However, when Percival himself saw (in 1946) the translated Japanese transcript of his surrender conversation, he commented: 'Although there are elements of fact in it, parts of it are quite fictitious. It presumably comes from a Japanese source and like all their publications, is highly coloured. No reliability should be placed on it as an official document.'

Yamashita's conquest was despite Sir Winston Churchill's firm (if unrealistic) orders from London on 20 January to the beleaguered British military HQ within Fort Canning Hill's underground bunker.

'I want to make it absolutely clear that I expect every inch of ground to be defended, every scrap of material or defences to be blown to pieces to prevent capture by the enemies, and no question of surrender to be entertained until after protracted

Tom Stoppard Escapes

One of the civilian boats fleeing Singapore for India in February 1942 had on board a little boy who would grow up to become the noted playwright/screenwriter, Tom Stoppard. His father (of Jewish origin) had fled Nazified Czechoslovakia in 1939 for what he imagined was the safety of Singapore. Only in his own case, no. Stoppard's father sent his family to safety, but he himself died here 'in enemy hands'.

fighting among the ruins of Singapore city.' At the time of issuing these stern words, Churchill was unaware that the island was not the 'Fortress Singapore' of British official propaganda. More like the 'Naked Island'.

Or, as the ditty composed by 'Pinkie' Evans of the Manchester Regiment went: 'Singapore, mighty fortress / Guardian of the East / The Japanese didn't think so / They took it in a week.'

Churchill was also presumably unaware of the lack of perception behind the words of then British Governor Sir Shenton Thomas. When awoken by an early-morning phonecall on 8 December from Gen Percival giving the shock news of the Japanese landings in Kelantan, Sir Shenton is quoted as replying: 'Well, I suppose you'll shove the little men off!'

'Well, I suppose you'll shove the little men off!' ...

After February 1942, Yamashita (then a 56-year-old) should have been able to wallow in his military glow, his name should have been uttered with awe back in the imperial capital of Tokyo. Yet before his 'glory year' had run even half its course, he was yanked out of Singapore in semi-disgrace and ordered to the military wasteland of northern Manchuria. Without visiting Tokyo on the way either, meaning, with severe loss of face.

Yamashita was thus not to see his Emperor in person to present his Malayan victory report, as he felt he deserved to. What had led to this almighty tumble?

A political gaffe on 29 April 1942 at the old Adelphi Hotel, behind City Hall and facing the Padang (now covered by Adelphi Shopping Centre), was technically the reason. Yet what might be called 'office politics' was at the root of it all.

For during the 1920s/early 1930s, Yamashita had unwisely made a political enemy in the shape of General Hideki Tojo, who as War Minister would launch the Japanese military offensive before becoming Japan's wartime Prime Minister. Even while he was storming through Malaya, 'Tiger' sourly noted in his diary: 'It is bad that Japan has no one in high places who can be relied upon. Most men abuse their power ...'

A Crucial Slip of the Tongue

Yamashita's 'gaffe' at the Adelphi was mildly surprising, as he was said to be a politically shrewd man. The order had gone out that a major ceremony was required for 29 April, the Emperor's birthday. A march of schoolchildren would be organised through the city's streets, during which they would each carry a Japanese flag and sing a patriotic song called 'Aikoku Koshin Kyoku' – or 'Look at the Dawn over the Eastern Seas'.

This was in contrast to another requirement of Singapore's children under Japanese rule. Whenever they passed a sentry, they were to bow their heads as low as they could and wish them 'Konbanwa' or 'Good day'. Only that Japanese word sounded just too much like the abusive Malay term 'Chium bawah' for the temptation to be resisted.

After their parade through the streets, the children were expected to gather on the Padang while Yamashita appeared on the City Hall balcony, when they would sing Japan's national anthem and shout 'Banzai!' ('Long live the Emperor!') three times.

The children divided into two groups, converging on the Padang from Orchard Road and from Chinatown. At 10 am, Yamashita appeared on the balcony. The singing commenced. It was said that Yamashita was so moved by the rows and rows of young singing voices – 'Just like Japanese children, aren't they?', he was overheard to remark – that tears started to run down his broad face.

The children moved off, their job done. Yamashita and his party moved next door to the Adelphi Hotel where he was to meet and 'receive the loyalty' of grown-up Singaporeans. Clearly still moved by the occasion, Yamashita uttered his fateful *Fateful words ...* words: 'Today, we celebrate the Emperor's birthday with you. You have just become our new subjects … I want the people of Malaya and Sumatra to carry on with their affairs, for they are now our new subject people.'

'Subject people', is it? This may have be the actual truth, but it hardly fitted in with the official Japanese propaganda of 'liberating' the oppressed peoples of east and south Asia from their oppressive European masters and 'inviting' them to join Japan's Greater Asia Co-Prosperity Sphere.

Tojo Okays Brothels

Hideki Tojo was posthumously shown to have had a hand in what postwar Japan officially denied: setting up brothels abroad with local women forced into sex slavery to service victorious Japanese troops.

In 1992, a telegram was unearthed in Tokyo. Dated 12 March 1942, it had been sent by a senior army official in Taiwan for Tojo's personal attention. It asked: 'Regarding a request I have received from South Theatre Head-quarters to dispatch 50 comfort natives to Borneo, I ask your permission to send the following three selected by the military police as brothel managers.' Tojo signed his approval.

Japanese journalists rushed Yamashita's remarks back to their home newspapers, and Yamashita's domestic political enemies seized upon them to make sure his goose was truly cooked. Especially Tojo.

Within weeks, Field Marshal Count Terauchi, who was Supreme Commander of Japanese troops for the region, arrived in Singapore and took up residence in Government House (today's Istana). Yamashita already had reason to loathe this soft-living aristocrat. After the Count (rather than Yamashita) had awarded some campaign medals locally, 'Tiger' fumed in his diary: 'That bloody Terauchi. He's been living in Saigon, with a comfortable bed, good food, and playing Japanese chess!'

Exile to Manchuria

It was Terauchi who passed on Tojo's 'you're fired' message to Yamashita. And Tojo's order that he take up the military command in Manchuria. Speedily, too, staying in Singapore for only as long as it took to wrap up the $50 million 'voluntary contribution' Japan had demanded from the region's Chinese communities. Yamashita's final public appearance in Singapore came on the morning of 25 June 1942 at Fullerton Building (the Japanese Military Command HQ, ex-GPO and imminent Fullerton Hotel), where he received the money so reluctantly collected by the Overseas Chinese Association under its even more reluctant president, the distinguished Lim Boon Keng.

The collection hadn't quite reached the $50 million mark. Yamashita received $28.75 million in cash, with the balance of $21.25 million being pledged through a Yokohama bank loan at 6% annual interest for a term of one year. Ten million of the original $50 million had been demanded from Singapore's Chinese; the rest from the Chinese in Malaya's various states, according to their size and prosperity.

Yamashita's 'final curtain' speech lasted over an hour. He expounded upon the reasons for the war and on, as he saw it, the moral and spiritual superiority of the Japanese race. They were, he argued, descended from the gods. This was unlike the Europeans who, he maintained, had descended from monkeys – as Charles Darwin had proved so conclusively! And if there was a war between gods and monkeys, then obviously 'even a fool could see who would win'. With this final piece of evolutionary 'lesson', it was time for 'Tiger' to pack up and go.

An evolutionary 'lesson' …

Yamashita went straight to Manchuria via Taiwan, or Formosa as it was then called. Sympathetic Japanese officers arranged for three of the island's choicest geisha girls to spend the stopover night with him to help soothe his wounded pride. He politely declined the offer, and went to bed alone.

Yamashita's next major military assignment came in October 1944 when he was rushed to the Philippines as Commander-in-Chief. But the tide of war had turned by then and militarily, it was too late for Yamashita to make any effective difference.

Tojo's Teeth

Hideki Tojo was hanged – following a failed suicide attempt – on 23 December 1948 after a war crimes tribunal had branded him as the individual most responsible for Japan's insane aggressions. Tojo went to his gallows unknowingly wearing 'doctored' false teeth. He'd requested a new set to help him speak more clearly during his trial. The American dentist (a Dr George Foster) assigned to this job used the Morse code dots and dashes to engrave the message 'Remember Pearl Harbour' on Tojo's dentures.

Tojo is buried at the Yasukuni Shrine in central Tokyo, which is regarded as 'housing the spirits' of Japan's 2.6 million war dead. Annual official visits by senior right-wing Japanese politicians to this nationalist shrine to 'war heroes' (including many war criminals) continue to provoke controversy.

American forces had surged back to the Philippines that year with a huge invading force under General Douglas MacArthur and retaken Manila by February 1945. The two A-bombs dropped on Japan in August 1945 rendered further struggle meaningless. The image-obsessed MacArthur accepted the Japanese surrender from a tearful Yamashita on 1 September 1945. Five weeks later, MacArthur demanded personal retribution for the deaths of 150 American PoWs. Oh, and for the estimated 100,000 Filipino civilians slaughtered by the Japanese in and around Manila in a series of frenzied massacres when they realised they had no hope.

MacArthur wanted Yamashita's thick neck. 'Tiger' had to pay the price, even though he argued at his trial that he had not organised or even known about the civilian atrocities. Indeed, he claimed, he had expressly forbidden last-ditch Japanese fighting in Manila, which he had officially vacated and declared an 'open city'.

It was, he insisted, MacArthur's egoistical urge to stage a de Gaulle-style triumphant return march into Manila and get installed in its Malacanang Palace by his birthday on 26 January that had left the 16,000-strong Japanese garrison seeing no

Yamashita Road?

Yamashita's name nearly made it (if temporarily) into Singapore's *Street Directory*. In early 1942, his senior colleagues had wanted to rename Stamford Road in his honour. The Tiger declined. One central Singapore road name-change was made as soon as the Occupation ended in September 1945. Japan Street was wiped off the map to become today's Boon Tat Street, where Lau Pa Sat food stalls are now put out as darkness falls.

Yamashita's Treasure

One last mystery refused to die with 'Tiger'. Was there such a thing as 'Yamashita's Treasure' and what happened to it? This treasure is the horde he was alleged to have plundered from rich men's homes as his spoils of victory in Malaya and Singapore, with 'souvenirs' from Thailand and Burma also – gold, precious jewellery, valuable paintings, select objects d'art, and so on.

Insistence upon the horde's existence lingers on most strongly in the Philippines, where it was said that treasure worth some $300 million was hidden in 172 secret locations around that country's many islands.

It was even alleged by Imelda Marcos that her deceased and disgraced husband Ferdinand, far from stripping the Philippine treasury bare for his own personal use, was an independently wealthy man through his 'discovery' of Yamashita's Treasure.

It has since emerged that Marcos had in 1972 ordered Philippine troops to dig a series of 40 m-deep holes across the country in an elaborate – and phoney – Yamashita Treasure hunt. For Marcos was aiming to give the impression that the loot found in these 'post-dated' holes were actually the original source of his wealth. After his 1986 downfall, Philippine investigators established that the primary source of his gold was what he'd looted from Manila's central bank – ruling that Marcos had been 'a fantastic liar'.

But a Japanese-American businessman named Minoru Fukumitsu, who had served as one of Gen MacArthur's war crimes investigators, had undertaken a widespread and fruitless hunt for the treasure. He'd struck a deal with the new Philippines administration to use his insights and contacts to investigate the horde's existence, in exchange for the release of 200 Japanese PoWs. But officially, no luck.

How about Singapore's MacRitchie Reservoir: did Yamashita stash his goodies there? In 1981, an Indonesian gardener named Sappari, who had worked at the reservoir during the Occupation years, suggested that something very valuable had been buried close to the Jinja shrine. His story went that just before defeat looked imminent in 1945, several Japanese soldiers in trucks drove up to the reservoir and undertook what Sappari described as 'a lot of activity'.

In 1947, the British administration had hired Sappari and seven other labourers to dig deep at the suspect end of the reservoir, paying them a sizeable sum for their efforts – and their secrecy. Sappari commented (in 1981): 'It was hard work. We worked on several spots, digging a total of 21 holes to a depth of some seven metres. But we found nothing.'

Then there's Batam and other neighbouring Riau islands in Indonesia. It was said that several high-ranking Japanese officers got out of Singapore just ahead of the British in 1945 and hid out awhile on these nearby islands, together with a large slice of Yamashita's Treasure. Who knows?

Actually, if there ever was such a horde of valuable wartime booty, it would most probably have found its way back to Japan. And that nation's secretive ways would mean that the real truth about Yamashita's Treasure will never be known ...

option but to fight back in a suicidal desperation that degenerated into ghastly slaughters of Manila's civilians.

This defence was not accepted; Yamashita was found guilty. On 7 December 1945 – exactly four years after the Pearl Harbour bombings and Kelantan landings – he was sentenced to death.

Yamashita's Last Days

Some observers such as the author of Yamashita's English-language biography *A Soldier Must Hang*, John Deane Potter, argued that his death sentence was a 'judicial lynching'. But Yamashita himself didn't query the verdict. As far as he was concerned, he and Japan had lost the war – so he and Japan had to face the consequences. As he saw it, his only 'crime' was being on the losing side.

Yet Yamashita would surely have encountered the same fate if he'd faced trial in Singapore. Under British law, he could have been held responsible for the killing of British subjects – most noticeably, of course, those thousands of Chinese who disappeared in Operation Sweep-Up and at other stages during the Occupation.

Yamashita was interviewed in his death cell by Potter. He found the man Filipinos had dubbed 'Old Potato Face' in a rueful mood. He'd composed this

'Old Potato Face' ...

short poem: 'The world I knew is now a shameful place / There will never come a better time / For me to die.'

Among the tokens he had at his end was something from that glory period in Singapore when it seemed nothing and no one could stop Japan. It was an Australian Occupation bank note, a sample of the currency Japan intended to introduce after it had conquered Australia.

Yamashita was hanged at Los Banos in Laguna, south of Manila, at 5.59 am on 26 February 1946 – close to four years after his humiliation of Percival in the Ford boardroom. Facing his gallows, he straightened his shoulders, bowed in the direction of Tokyo and uttered his final words: 'I pray for the Emperor's long life and his prosperity for ever.'

Good as Gold

Tiger Lager Beer
Asia Pacific Breweries, Tuas

A Tiger roars into life, leaping from local brew
to 'world's best beer' ...

In 1932, Singapore's beer drinkers were first able to fill their
mugs and jugs with a locally-brewed lager. For then Tiger
roared into life from Malayan Breweries on Alexandra Road,
an enterprise set up the year before by Fraser & Neave in
cooperation with the Amsterdam-based lager giant Heineken.

This tie-up happened almost by accident. Heineken had
come out to these parts looking to set up a brewery in Indonesia
(then a Dutch colony). This did not work out but when the
disappointed homebound Heineken export manager was
stopping over in the Raffles Hotel, he bumped into a senior
F&N executive.

The two men agreed that Singapore was worth a go – and
within months, brewing masters, barley and hops, yeast,
brewing machinery experts, quality control tasters and training
staff all came from the Netherlands to Singapore. Clearly, in
this matter, F&N believed in going Dutch. The aim was to fire
up its Tiger with all the expertise Heineken could transfer to
the Far East.

It didn't take long for rival German brewer Beck's (home
base: Bremen) to hear the roar. Soon Beck's had set up
Archipelago Brewery (also on Alexandra Road) where it
produced Anchor lager beer, pitching it at a slightly lower
price – a marketing strategy still in place today.

Then in 1939, with the outbreak of World War II,
Archipelago was snatched by the 'Custodian of Enemy
Property'. In 1941, Malayan Breweries bought out Archipelago
– though with the Netherlands then under Nazi occupation,

that Custodian was just a little anxious about the deal. Never mind: by 1945, the local beer competition had assumed its still rather phoney nature.

The Tiger Leaps Forward

The postwar strides of Tiger were relentless as it made itself a Singapore brand name as strong as the likes of Tiger Balm, Axe Oil, Amoy, Yeo's, Three Rifles, even F&N's own Orange Crush. In 1955, the South Pacific Brewery in Papua New Guinea was acquired; one year later, so was New Zealand's Leopard Brewery.

Increased demand saw a separate brewery opened in Kuala Lumpur in 1962, and in 1983 big-drinking Papua New Guinea's other brewery was gobbled up. In cooperation with Indonesia's Bintang brewers (now mostly owned by Heineken), Tiger was produced from Surabaya in 1984 for Irian Jaya and then from 1991 for wider Indonesian distribution. A further joint venture based in Ho Chi Minh City launched Tiger for the Vietnamese market, where its early adverts using statuesque Caucasian females allegedly led to Vietnam banning foreign faces from its local advertising. In Cambodia, Tiger is now the favoured prestige imported beer, while clever new adverts showing the Great Wall of China made up of Tiger carton 'bricks' marked the lager's arrival in China's huge market.

In 1989, the Malaysian stout operation was merged with that of Guinness, so that the two local dark beers – Guinness and ABC – came under the same umbrella to launch their equally rather phoney stout wars, and to easily outpace imported contenders such as Copenhagen's Royal Stout. And to produce Singapore's sexiest coffeeshop poster adverts, alluringly using TV actresses such as Jazreel Low and Aileen Tan to further promote the Stout cause.

New Stripes for the Tiger

The Big Bang in the regional brewing world came in 1990 with a new overall company being created under the name Asia Pacific Breweries. Then in May that year, the new $200 million Tiger Brewery at Tuas was officially opened on a nine-hectare site using the 'most technologically advanced facility in the Asia-Pacific region' while still getting its most important basic ingredient – fresh water – from Johor. A Heineken team from Amsterdam had helped in its design and supervision, renewing the strong links established back in 1931.

Tiger lager now dominates these beer-drinking parts, and the Gold Medal boast on its label is not a hollow one. Indeed, it has collected at least 25 such medals – and just before Tiger's 50th anniversary in 1981, a UK **Tiger on top ...** experts' blind tasting of 32 reputed international lagers saw Tiger come out on top with an 80% overall approval rating.

While in 1988, at what, with typical American zeal, was tagged the 'World's Number One Beer Contest' at Washington DC's Brickskeller restaurant, Tiger roared through the blind tastings to win gold.

The World's Very Best Lagers

Actually, the very best lager beers are brewed in the Czech Republic. Most notably, Pilsner Urquell and the original Budweiser (which was unable to protect its famous name and thus prevent American pale imitators from making their own Budweiser).

Pilsner Urquell simply means 'original Pilsner', alluding to both its Czech home region and its 'bottom-fermentation' brewing method. A leading beer guidebook described Urquell as 'an immensely complex beer'.

This was enough for Singapore's annual official handbook, which now lists Tiger as 'world's best beer', alongside the nation's other achievements such as the Shangri-La as the world's best business hotel, Changi as the world's best airport, PSA as world's busiest container port, and the like.

Singapore's appetite for beer, home-brewed and imported, is ever-growing. In 1992, 7,388,735 decalitres (10 litres) were downed – one million up on the previous year's figure, and including a suspiciously precise statistic of 9% (numbering 98,000) for the proportion of women among the nation's beer-drinkers.

Tiger keeps a sharp eye on beer trends, pouncing as and when necessary. In 1992, it came out with Raffles Light (a name which at the time offended Raffles Hotel) for the

A sharp eye on beer trends ...

female/health-alert market. The next year, sprang forth the weighty Tiger Classic for the premium/yuppie market. And in 1998, the newest cub in the Tiger family, Baron's Strong Brew (launched in 1996) also struck gold. It scooped the champion prize in the International Strong Beer category at the 1998 Brewing Industry Awards held in London. At this same event, Tiger beer itself achieved possibly its greatest accolade to date – by beating off 191 international competitors to win the Gold Medal in the International Lager Category. Tiger has seen beer fads such as Mexican beers drunk from the bottle, Swedish dark-brews, Japanese 'dry' beers and Canadian 'ice-brewed' beer come and go – and has not been afraid.

For Tiger itself now prowls widely abroad, exporting 50% of its beer to some 50 countries. Bold Tiger beer print adverts show dreamy views of noted world beauty spots and proclaim: 'Good as gold around the world.' Meaning that Asia Pacific Breweries face the future with confidence, with its Tiger! Tiger! burning bright. It's a long way from those Dutch master-brewers seeing what might happen if they transplanted the Heineken method to the tropics ...

The Tiger's Kick

Tiger Beer played a major part in establishing Singapore's S-League domestic professional football tournaments and is still the biggest single sponsor of Singapore soccer. And the biennial Tiger Cup is now the biggest soccer event in Southeast Asia, with ten nations keenly taking part.

What's even better, Singapore won this trophy (and $136,800) in September 1998 by beating home team Vietnam 1-0! And that after the now infamous semi-final match between Thailand and Indonesia which both teams strove so hard to lose. But despite his nickname, ace part-Thai golfer Tiger Woods is *not* sponsored by Singapore's sporty lager ...

Anthony Burgess's Tiger

Tiger lager beer has achieved an impressive literary status. This came courtesy of that tiger of the written word, Anthony Burgess, who had over 50 literary works to his name (most notably, the novels *Earthly Powers* and *A Clockwork Orange*). This highly opinionated and sometimes pompous wordsmith died of cancer in 1993 (still indignant that he never did win a Nobel Prize for Literature).

In 1956, at 39 years of age, his first novel appeared under the title *Time for a Tiger*. He did indeed mean the beer. That was then its advertising slogan! This novel was the first in what Burgess would package as *A Malayan Trilogy*. The threesome is now marketed as *The Long Day Wanes. Time for a Tiger* concerned itself with British and other immigrants working, complaining and boozing in an unspecified Malayan state.

The novels sprang from the six years Burgess spent as an education officer in the British Colonial Service in then British North Borneo and Malaya until returning to the UK for health reasons in 1959, where he soon took to full-time writing.

Flying high – a huge balloon in the shape of a can of Tiger Beer.

Some bookish statistics that may impress markers of A-Level English Literature exam essays: The 16th sentence Burgess ever had published ended as follows: '... thirst for a warmish bottle of Tiger beer.' By a similar count, that phrase 'bottle of Tiger beer' marked the 151st–154th (inclusive) words this extremely prolific writer had published.

Now, a vivid account of the beer's central status in a white man's Malaya (from *Time for a Tiger*): 'I'll take my dying Bible that if it was the Day of Judgement itself and the dead coming out of their graves and we all of us lined up for the bloody sentence and He in His awe and majesty as of a flame of fire standing in the clouds of doomsday, all you'd be thinking about would be where you could get a bottle of blasted Tiger.'

Given that Asia Pacific spent S$3.6 million advertising Tiger in 1993, it's mildly surprising that the brewery has never exploited the sophisticated cultural status of Anthony Burgess for promoting its beer. Such adverts would be far less irritating than those plastic-glossy TV images of affluent Caucasians at play, as if there was something visually inferior about local faces enjoying their Tigers. Grrr, a sting in the tale?

The End of a Movement

The grave of Tan Chay Wa, Chinese Buddhist section, Chua Chu Kang Cemetery, Choa Chu Kang Road and his small part in the activities of the Communist Party of Malaya (CPM)

In 1983, an inscribed tombstone sparked off a court case that eventually made the pages of London's The Sunday Times ...

It may be said that Tan Chay Wa continues his violent political struggle from beyond the grave. Chay Wa was a Singapore bus driver who was arrested on 2 July 1979 at a Kulai vegetable farm, just off the Johor Bahru-Air Hitam highway. He had a .32 Llama semi-automatic pistol and seven rounds of bullets in his possession. Chay Wa, a member of the Malayan National Liberation Front (subservient to the Communist Party of Malaya), was duly convicted under Malaysia's severe British-inherited Internal Security Act and given the mandatory death sentence by Johor Bahru's High Court.

On 18 January 1983 at 35 years of age, Chay Wa was hanged in Kuala Lumpur's Pudu Prison, after which his body was brought back across the Causeway. In the Chua Chu Kang's Chinese Buddhist cemetery, his tombstone told the story of his short life, and his turbulent inner emotions as his execution drew near. It told this story in Chinese characters.

Story of a short life ...

If they could be read, that is. For most of them have been whited out with plaster. This cover-up was carried out in 1985 by, it was reported, members of Tan's own family who wished to obscure any glorification of his 'martyrdom' in the communist cause. They did an effective job. Though some of the white plaster has come off – or has been scraped off – over the years, the message underneath is indeed obscured. All that can be clearly seen is a photograph of Tan and some lettering that gives his name and the years of his birth and death.

It is, however, known exactly what the covered-up lettering says. The full details emerged from a 1983 court case when the dead man's brother, Tan Chu Boon (then a 40-year-old tropical fish breeder), was convicted on charges arising from the tombstone's lettering and sentenced to one year in jail. This was later reduced on appeal to one month.

Chu Boon had argued in court that he himself was not a communist nor did he in fact have political leanings of any kind; that he had not monitored or even read the words for the proposed tombstone inscription; and that these words had been handed to him on a piece of paper by his brother's widow to give to the tombstone inscriber. These arguments the court refused to accept.

In translation, the tombstone inscription had described Tan as a 'martyr from a poor peasant family' who had conducted his political work 'in total disregard of his own personal safety', while showing 'the noble quality of a revolutionary warrior'.

After Chay Wa's arrest and during his subsequent imprisonment, continued the (lengthy) inscription, he was 'cruelly beaten up and subjected to coercive threats and inducement but he remained resolute and unflinchingly dauntless' before his 'heroic death'.

It then noted that just before his death, Chay Wa had written a poem. It gave this verse in full: 'With heart filled with righteous indignation, I stand at the gallows and forcefully pen this poem with blood. I want to air my grievances for a hundred years, unable to tell all the wrongs with blood. When will this gallows be destroyed to bring about a new heaven?'

The tombstone inscription finished by noting: 'This militant poem depicts his hatred against the old society and his boundless confidence in the victory of the motherland's revolution. His glorious image will forever live in the minds of the people. Martyr Tan Chay Wa's spirit will live forever!'

In local communist parlance, that term 'motherland' referred to Peninsula Malaysia and Singapore as one unified political entity and 'liberation cause' referred to communist attempts to overthrow the established governments through armed struggle.

Yet as noted by British author Dennis Bloodworth in his book *The Tiger and the Trojan Horse*, these tombstone words 'were proof that this was the epitaph of a man, not a movement'. That movement's epitaph was to come just six years later ...

The Trial of Tan Chay Wa

At his November 1983 trial, Tan Chu Boon said that he and other family members had visited his brother in KL the night before his execution, after which they had brought his body back to Singapore where they had him buried on 20 January. At the Chua Chu Kang cemetery, Tan was approached by one of those engravers who 'work on site' and $1,800 was the agreed price for an inscribed tombstone.

After Tan had handed over the desired words on a piece of paper, the engraver warned that there might be 'trouble' because of the wording. He claimed in court that Tan had checked the final script before approving it and saying it would be his (Tan's) business if there was any comeback from the authorities.

The court then heard that the CID Secret Society Investigation Branch was called into the case on 11 May and had seized the original piece of paper from the tombstone-maker's shop in Chua Chu Kang. Tan Chu Boon had then been arrested at his Boon Lay Drive flat on 28 May.

Tan's defence lawyer was J.B. (Ben) Jeyaretnam who has himself long been a consistent thorn in the side of Singapore's political establishment. Mr Jeyaretnam established that the instigation for the CID investigation had come from 'a government department'.

One of the charges on which Mr Tan was found guilty was that he had 'under his control, the tombstone of his brother, Tan Chay Wa, on which was engraved in Chinese characters an inscription which tended to advocate acts prejudicial to the security of Singapore'. The court threw out the defence plea that this inscription was nothing more than an attempt to praise the 'noble qualities' of Chay Wa, and that they could not in any way be interpreted as a 'call to take up arms against the government'.

In mitigation, Mr Jeyaretnam had made the point that, apart from immediate family and friends, no one else would have known about the tombstone and its inscription.

It is indeed difficult to track down the Chay Wa grave at No 3222 in Block 8, near the junction of Chinese Cemetery paths 14 and 20. For it stands in a huge sea of tombstones that stretch almost as far as the eye can see in every direction. Only those purposely looking for it are likely to find the 'subversive' tombstone.

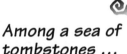

Among a sea of tombstones ...

The CID action against his older brother had one unintended consequence – it made Chay Wa much better-known than he may otherwise have deserved. For it led to London's *The Sunday Times* newspaper taking up the story a few months after the 1983 trial, making the case an internationally-known (if short-lived) issue and depicting the Singapore government in a decidedly hostile manner. Robust 'don't interfere in our internal affairs' retorts soon emerged from government circles.

Death of a Cause

The formal acknowledgement that the cause for which Tan Chay Wa had sacrificed his life was itself dead came on 2 December 1989. Then the Communist Party of Malaya (CPM) signed two separate pacts during a 30-minute 'peace session' in the southern Thai town of Haadyai with government representatives of Malaysia and Thailand. This recognised that the 'War of the Running Dogs' (which had started in Perak in June 1948) was finally over, that the 1,188 remaining active CPM guerillas would lay down their arms, obey local laws and pledge loyalty to the two nations who, in their turn, would 'provide fair treatment to these members'.

Among the CPM ranks at this time were 21 Singaporeans; 494 Malaysians (402 Chinese, 77 Malays, 13 Orang Asli – jungle aborigines – and two Indians); 670 Thais (479 Muslims, 184 Chinese, seven ethnic); one Indonesian and even two Japanese veterans of the Pacific War who had joined the CPM after their country's surrender in 1945 and who were now requesting permission from Tokyo to return to Japan.

Signing the CPM surrender-that-was-not-a-surrender was Chin Peng, a man who surely deserved the tag 'colourful character'. For he had taken over the CPM *A 'colourful character'* ... reins in 1947 and directed its urban and rural guerilla activities ever since. Chin Peng had come to Singapore as a 6-year-old and was educated at Chinese High School and St Andrew's before becoming a crime reporter with a now-defunct Chinese newspaper.

His brave anti-Japanese guerilla activities in Malaya from 1943–45 had won him an OBE medal from a grateful Britain and an invitation to London to attend the post-war Victory Parade. When, however, the War of the Running Dogs got underway, Chin Peng was stripped of his OBE and fled Singapore (he was last seen here in 1950) with a price on his head. He spent most of the intervening years in the Malayan jungles or southern Thailand, with some time spent in Beijing and on Indonesia's Bintan island.

So his reappearance in December 1989 provoked much media interest. Then 67, he described himself as still a 'Marxist-Leninist' but one journalist chose to describe him as looking 'more like a successful businessman than a revolutionary'.

Speaking in Malay, Chin Peng finally officially stated the CPM's recognition of Singapore as a independent nation, thus dropping its 'motherland' policy. He pledged further that the remnants of his movement would 'not interfere in the internal affairs of other countries'. What's more, he promised: 'We shall disband our armed units and destroy our weapons to show our sincerity to terminate the armed struggle.'

'An honourable settlement, not a surrender,' he pleaded. Chin Peng had actually got himself and his band of merry men (plus some women) a good deal, given the weakness of their position in an utterly-changed, post-communist world.

In a 1990 *Shin Min Daily News* interview expressing a hope that he could come back 'one day' to lead a normal life in Singapore, Chin Peng said he would personally welcome the chance to 'contribute to Singapore's stability, prosperity and progress' as he had 'made so few contributions, if any, to Singapore – or maybe it is just that I couldn't'.

The Plen

Senior Minister Lee Kuan Yew gave Chin Peng his familiar nickname, The Plen – short for plenipotentiary, meaning a fully-authorised emissary. Mr Lee met The Plen four times before the turning-point 1959 Singapore general election, then once in 1961. Following a 1958 meeting, Mr Lee described The Plen as 'pale, never seen sunshine for years, on the run' – but still in charge of the CPM.

For his part, The Plen described Lee Kuan Yew as 'one of the most incorruptible statesmen in Asia'.

At Haadyai, much media interest had inevitably focused on Singapore-born Miss Huang Hui Her, whom Chin Peng described as his 'longtime personal secretary'. But apart from stating that she was in her 40s and had studied at Singapore's Nanyang University, she frustratingly did not disclose any further personal details. When last heard of, Hui Her was in Beijing where Chin Peng was said to be dictating his memoirs to her.

After the peace treaty had been signed, Thailand's chief signatory (then Acting Supreme Commander General Chavalit Yongchaiyudh) nominated 2 December 1989 as a 'Day of Peace' –

A 'Day of Peace' ...

one on which it had been finally recognised that 'differences and problems could not be resolved through the use of force'.

A Last Controversial Link

There's one individual in Singapore who represents a controversial link with the bygone communist-clouded days – Chia Thye Poh, who failed by just three years to equal the 'record' set by South African President Nelson Mandela as the world's longest-serving political prisoner.

Mr Chia was arrested in October 1966 under Singapore's equally severe and also British-inherited Internal Security Act for his alleged involvement with the CPM. Mr Chia was then 25 years of age and an abstaining Barisan Sosialis (Socialist Party) MP for Jurong. He was finally released in May 1989, though freedom would have come much earlier if he had 'renounced' the CPM. His stubborn position was, however, that as he never was a CPM member, he thus had nothing to renounce.

His release conditions were extraordinary: he was to stay full-time in a small house alongside the Fort Siloso monorail station on the 'family fun island' of Sentosa.

After that CPM peace agreement session in 1989, these conditions of exile were loosened so that Mr Chia could visit and remain on mainland Singapore from 6 am – 9 pm daily. When informed in September 1990 of these new conditions, Mr Chia was far from grateful. He said: 'I don't feel particularly excited about it as I think the Government should have released me unconditionally.' He said one of his first 'mainland' priorities was to visit his family members living in Ang Mo Kio.

And in November 1998, all restrictions on Chia Thye Poh were finally lifted. He commented: 'Now I can live the life of an ordinary citizen. The restriction order should have been lifted long ago. I am nearly 58 years old already. It has been a long time, 32 years – the best part of my life is gone.'

From Sentosa Mr Chia would have had a sweeping view of the skyscrapers of Singapore's financial district, its so-busy 24-hour port, its swish city-centre hotels, its lavish East Coast condos. Together with Orchard Road shopping centres, designer boutiques, karaoke lounges, Michael Jackson concerts, Channel 8 drama serials, pagers, handphones, foreign holidays, Coca-Cola, COEs, ERP gantries and Y2K bugs (plus the theme park attractions of Sentosa itself), they point to the direction the government and people of Singapore have chosen to follow since independence. And to why the CPM's efforts over a 40-year period proved in the end to be such a military, political and social failure …

About the Author

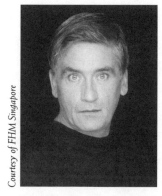

Courtesy of FHM Singapore

Dublin-born Londoner David Brazil arrived in Singapore during August 1988 – to discover that this was an extremely auspicious month (8-88) and that he was just days ahead of the handphone's arrival.

He accepts that since then, the mobile phone has hugely outpaced his own impact on Singapore but he has happily spent his years here on journalism, books, photographing, part-time modelling and acting, all sorts. His local enthusiasms include cats, cooking, clubbing, cycling and some things not beginning with the letter 'c' ...

Index